TWAYNE'S WORLD AUTHORS SERIES

A Survey of the World's Literature

Sylvia E. Bowman, Indiana University

GENERAL EDITOR

SPAIN

Gerald Wade, Vanderbilt University
Janet W. Díaz, University of North Carolina, Chapel Hill

EDITORS

Rosalía de Castro

TWAS 446

Rosalía de Castro

ROSALÍA DE CASTRO

By KATHLEEN KULP-HILL

Eastern Kentucky University

TWAYNE PUBLISHERS

A DIVISION OF G. K. HALL & CO., BOSTON

Library of Congress Cataloging in Publication Data
Kulp-Hill, Kathleen.
  Rosalía de Castro.

  (Twayne's world authors series ; TWAS 446 :
Spain)
  Bibliography: p. 137–43.
  Includes index.
  1. Castro, Rosalía de, 1837–1885. 2. Authors,
Spanish—19th century—Biography. 3. Authors,
Gallegan—19th century—Biography.
PQ6512.C226Z7   861'.5   76-58860
ISBN 0-8057-6282-5

To TLH

Contents

About the Author

Kathleen Kulp-Hill studied at Kansas State University and at the University of New Mexico, where she received the Ph. D. in 1967. She has taught Spanish and Portuguese at the University of Colorado and at Eastern Kentucky University, where she has been a member of the Department of Foreign Languages since 1969. The study of Portuguese at the University of New Mexico and in Brazil led to an interest in Galician literature, Rosalía de Castro, and medieval Galician-Portuguese poetry. She has previously published a comprehensive study of Rosalía's poetry (Kathleen K. Kulp, *Manner and Mood in Rosalía de Castro, a Study of Themes and Style*, Madrid: Ediciones José Porrua Turanzas, 1968).

Preface

Rosalía de Castro is not widely known outside the field of Spanish literature. Students of Spanish will remember her name and perhaps a few poems from a survey of literature course. At one time, not so very long ago, she would have been considered a minor though meritorious literary figure. More recent criticism selects her and Gustavo Adolfo Bécquer as the two best and most enduring poets of nineteenth-century Spain. Rosalía was in many respects ahead of her times, and certain facets of her work have received due appreciation only in later perspective. She is perennial and universal, with much to offer the twentieth-century reader.

Studies devoted to Rosalía and her works most often deal with her poetry, for which she is principally and deservedly known. The poetry itself is rarely treated as a whole, for she wrote in two languages—the dialect of her native Galicia (a living remnant of early Portuguese) and Castilian (i.e., Spanish). Hence, most audiences have had access to or interest in only those portions of her work in the language known to them. In addition to poetry, she wrote a considerable amount of prose, which is little known.

Two volumes of poetry have secured for Rosalía a place in Spanish literature: *Cantares gallegos (Galician Songs)*, in Galician; and *En las orillas del Sar (On the Banks of the River Sar)*, in Castilian. The first book coincided with the renewed cultural consciousness and political identity in Galicia in the nineteenth century and won for its author the fervent and lasting adoration of her fellow Galicians. The latter, her final published work, reached the larger audience of the Spanish-speaking world with its mature poetic voice.

In her own day Rosalía was an idol to the Galicians, but little noticed on the national (or Spanish) literary scene. Public taste was then enthralled by the more bombastic or pedantically philosophical poetry currently in vogue. The fame of many of the more "successful" poets passed with their times, however, and a later age has harkened to the exquisite lyricism and eternal themes of Rosalía. As a poet, she has come into her own, beloved by the writers of the Generation of 1898 and by succeeding literary movements, and has become the subject of ever-increasing critical attention.

It is apparent that Rosalía had serious aspirations as a novelist. Prose makes up a considerable portion of her work and, except for a few short pieces (a story and prefaces to poetic works), she wrote her prose in Castilian, addressing herself to a wide cosmopolitan audience. In prose, one might say, her timing was off. The late nineteenth century in Spain was a vigorous age of prose. Realism reigned, and its principal genre was the novel. Rosalía was contemporary with such great Spanish novelists as Fernán Caballero, Benito Pérez Galdós, Leopoldo Alas, and Emilia Pardo Bazán. In another age, or even at the beginning of the century, her prose might have received more attention. As it was, she was just another minor writer. With the objectivity of retrospect, however, her prose efforts can be seen to constitute an interesting aspect of the development of the Spanish novel, to express an integral part of Rosalía's literary personality, and to have sufficient literary merit to stand on their own.

It is the purpose of this volume to examine the literary production of Rosalía de Castro within the context of her life and times. All of her works are considered, at least briefly, with relatively more space devoted to the poetry because of its complexity and significance. The research and opinions of other Rosalian scholars have been consulted and cited, but the critical views represented in this study derive principally from my own experience with Rosalía's works. Chapter 1 presents perspectives on the century in which Rosalía lived. Chapter 2 deals with Galicia, Rosalía's immediate world and a region of strong cultural identity. Chapter 3 gives a biographical sketch. Chapters 4, 5, 6, and 7 are devoted to the poetry and include a brief summary of two early works, with a chapter on each of the major books. Chapter 8 discusses the prose works. The selected bibliography includes items considered most useful and accessible.

The translations of quotations from Rosalía and from other foreign sources are my own. I have attempted to convey accurately the meaning as well as the feeling of each passage. In the case of quotations from poetry, syntax and content of lines have been altered as little as possible, to allow for a more direct comparison with the original. The translations are intended as an aid to understanding rather than as poetic re-creations. No attempt has been made to preserve rhyme or meter; to seek to render these from Galician or Spanish into English would present great difficulties and interfere with the sense of the originals. The reader should keep in mind, however, that these elements are missing in the translations, and try to observe the sound and structure of Rosalía's text. Some notes to aid those unfamiliar with Galician are included in Chapter 5.

Acknowledgement is made to Aguilar, S. A. de Ediciones, Madrid, for their generous permission to quote from the *Obras Completas de Rosalía de Castro,* 6th ed., 1966. I wish also to express my appreciation to Dr. Gerald E. Wade, Dr. Sylvia E. Bowman, and Dr. Janet W. Díaz for their helpful guidelines and suggestions in the preparation of the manuscript. Special thanks are given to Dr. Margretta LeRoy for information and impressions gathered in Galicia, to Mrs. Leda Roitman for her reading and criticism of the manuscript, and to the many other friends and colleagues who lent their support and assistance to this effort.

KATHLEEN KULP-HILL

Eastern Kentucky University

Chronology

1837   Rosalía's birth is registered in the Hospital Real of Santiago de Compostela on February 24. This is generally considered the date of her birth.

1846   Separatist movement in Galicia against the Spanish government. A Supreme Governing Junta of Galicia is established. An insurrection in Carral is ruthlessly put down by General Narváez. Its leader, General Solís, and other patriots are executed.

1849   Publication of the first Realistic novel in Spain: *La gaviota* *(The Seagull)* by Cecilia Böhl de Faber [Fernán Caballero].

1856   Rosalía goes to Madrid to stay with a relative.

1857   Rosalía's first book, *La flor (The Flower)*, a collection of poems, is published in Madrid. It is reviewed in the periodical *La Iberia* by Manuel Murguía. Rosalía and Murguía announce their engagement.

1858   Rosalía de Castro and Manuel Murguía are married in Madrid on October 10.

1859   The Murguías' first child, Alejandra, is born in Santiago. Rosalía's first novel, *La hija del mar (Child from the Sea)*, is published in Vigo.

1861   A second novel, *Flavio*, is published in Madrid.

1862   Rosalía's mother, Doña Teresa de Castro y Abadía, dies.

1863   *Cantares gallegos (Galician Songs)*, a collection of folk-inspired poetry and Rosalía's first major work, is published in Vigo. A small volume of poetry, *A mi madre (To My Mother)*, also comes out in Vigo.

1866   Publication of the short story *"El cadiceño"* ("The Man from Cádiz") in Lugo, and of the novelette *Ruinas: desdichas de tres vidas ejemplares (Ruins: Misfortunes of Three Exemplary Lives)*, in Madrid.

1867   The novel *El caballero de las botas azules (The Gentleman of the Blue Boots)* is published in Lugo.

1868   Isabel II of Spain is deposed in the "Glorious Revolution"; Amadeo of Savoy succeeds her as king.

1869   The Murguías' second daugher, Aura, is born.

1870   Rosalía accompanies Murguía to Simancas on an official assignment in connection with his duties as government historian. There she begins to write the poems which will appear in *Follas novas (New Leaves)*. The Spanish poet Gustavo Adolfo Bécquer (born 1836) dies.

1871   *Rimas (Rhymes)* of Bécquer is published posthumously.

1871 or
1872   Twins, Gala and Ovidio, are born to Rosalía and Murguía.

1874   A daughter, Amara, is born to the Murguías.

1875   A son, Adriano Honorato Alejandro, is born.

1877   A daughter, Valentina, dies at birth.

1880   Rosalía's second major volume of poetry, *Follas novas (New Leaves)*, is published in Madrid.

1881   The novel *El primer loco (The First Madman)* is published in Madrid.

1884   Rosalía's last work and last major volume of poetry, *En las orillas del Sar (On the Banks of the River Sar)*, is published in Madrid.

1885   Rosalía dies of cancer on July 15 in the house called "La Matanza" in Padrón. She is buried in the nearby cemetery of Andina.

1891   Her remains are moved to the Convent of Santo Domingo de Bonaval in Santiago de Compostela.

1923   Manuel Murguía dies on February 2, at the age of ninety.

1964   Rosalía's last surviving child, Gala, dies at the age of ninety-three.

CHAPTER 1

Perspectives on the
Nineteenth Century in Spain

I   Historical Trends

ROSALÍA de Castro's life spanned forty-eight years of the
nineteenth century (1837–1885). Politically, this was a turbulent period for Spain. The century opened with the War of Independence, as the Spanish opposed Napoleon Bonaparte's attempt to
place his brother Joseph on the throne. The Spanish king, Fernando
VII, was restored, but a restless and often violent century ensued.
The legacy of the eighteenth century had been a fundamental,
polarized struggle of "the old" versus "the new"—or the traditional
Spanish values of Catholicism and monarchy and all that was "au-
thentically" Spanish bitterly pitted against the egalitarian, progres-
sive, and secular trends then taking hold in France, England, and
other parts of Europe and America. A chaotic succession of
monarchs, regents, military dictators, liberal uprisings, and short-
lived constitutions characterizes the century.

The Carlist Wars rent the country in civil strife, with the ab-
solutist, reactionary factions supporting Don Carlos, brother of Fernando VII, as rightful heir to the throne against Fernando's daughter, Isabel, who eventually became Queen Isabel II. The Spanish
Empire was severely reduced by the loss of the American colonies,
which won their independence early in the century. Attempts at
economic reform merely resulted in a change of masters for the
people, as the moneyed middle class supplanted church and aristocracy in the control of land and wealth. Outlying regions of distinct
cultural identity, especially Galicia, Catalonia, and the Basque Provinces, protested the policies of the centralized government and
made attempts to assert their own cultural and political autonomy.
As the century wore on, liberal attitudes and reforms made some
inroads, but never prevailed nor successfully compromised with

15

conservative factions. The century closed with the loss of the last remnants of empire to the United States in the Spanish-American War. Spain entered the twentieth century with its ideological conflicts still unresolved.

II *Literary Currents*

The nineteenth century was a rich period in Spanish literature. The movements of Romanticism and Realism dominated most of the century. The new esthetic currents of Modernism and the Generation of 1898 were stirring in the final years.

Romanticism, already victorious in France, England, and Germany at the end of the eighteenth and the beginning of the nineteenth centuries, entered Spain somewhat later with the return of young political exiles who had fled to France and England during the repressive reign of Fernando VII. New life was breathed into the rather stagnant cultural scene prevailing in Spain, where French influence and the Neo-Classical esthetics of the eighteenth century—control, discipline, restraint, and rationality—had always been somewhat alien. Romanticism represented, in a sense, a return to the earlier Spanish spirit, renewing links with the medieval and baroque past and unleashing the spontaneity, subjectivity, and creativity suppressed by Neo-Classicism.

Romanticism in Spain, as everywhere, was multiple and diverse in character. It pursued the ideal which could not compromise with imperfect reality, and gave vent to intense passion and ecstasy, or their opposites, pessimism and despair. Feeling took precedence over reason, and art tended to treat the exceptional and the elevated. There was great interest in the regional and the typical manifested in the collection and study of folklore and the literary genre termed *costumbrismo*, or the minute description and portrayal of local customs and characters. Another facet of Romanticism was the liberal spirit in politics and social reform, expressed literarily through criticism and satire, using the vehicles of the *costumbrista* sketch and journalism. Thus Romanticism accommodated the old as well as the new with its appreciation of the history, culture, and values of traditional Spain, as well as its search for individual freedom and expression and the goals of justice and equality.

The Romantic period in Spain was particularly rich in drama and poetry, which are the realms of passion, lyricism, and fantasy. Outstanding authors in these genres were José de Espronceda, Ángel Saavedra (the Duke of Rivas), and José Zorrilla. In the novel, historical adventure was favored, exemplified by Enrique Gil y Carrasco's *El señor de Bembibre* (The Lord of Benbibre). Vivid and witty *costumbrista* articles were produced by Ramón de Mesonero Romanos and Serafín Estébañez Calderón. Mariano José de Larra, with his mordant humor and profound perception, excelled as satirist and social critic.

By mid-century, the transition to Realism could be detected. The rebellious, youthful, self-centered spirit, incapable of reconciling the dream and the disappointment of daily existence, gave way to a more sober, objective confrontation with reality. Art focused on the humble, the familiar, the banal, even the sordid, stripping away the veil of illusion. Subjects were contemporary and immediate rather than distant in time or space. The middle and lower classes became material for plays, novels, and poems, and the city, its ways of life and its problems, entered the sphere of literature. This was the age of prose, and particularly of the novel. The minute observation of homely details practiced by the *costumbristas* evolved into a novelistic technique to create ambiance and character delineation. Interest in the regional persisted, and the various geographic areas and their cultural manifestations were studied for their determining influence on the life and attitudes of the inhabitants. The novel, in addition to telling stories, was an instrument of social criticism, keenly exposing injustice and hypocrisy and depicting the foibles and pathos of human nature. Psychological processes, the relation of childhood experiences and influences of surroundings to personality and behavior, were studied.

Naturalism, sequel to or outgrowth of Realism, existed in Spain only in modified form. The scientific examination of behavior in relation to heredity and environment, the preoccupation with the abnormal and the sordid, and the domination of man by his instincts, all of which characterized the Naturalistic novel, were mitigated by the basic Catholic belief in the free will and spiritual potential of the individual to combat the fate of his human condition. Idealism persisted and intensified the poignant awareness of the ironic contrast between human dreams and desires and human limitations and disappointments. It has been said that "every realist is a reformed idealist."[1] This must certainly apply to many of the great

Realistic novelists of Spain: Juan Valera; José María de Pereda; Armando Palacio Valdés; Emilia Pardo Bazán; Benito Pérez Galdós; and Leopoldo Alas, "Clarín."

Drama and poetry also manifested similar trends. Theater portrayed contemporary social situations and was written in prose, as exemplified by the plays of Adelardo López de Ayala, Manuel Tamayo y Baus, and José Echegaray. Poetry descended from the clouds and cultivated commonplace, ideological, or patriotic themes. Public taste admired the low key philosophy of Ramón del Campoamor and the ringing tones of Gaspar Núñez de Arce. Two delicately sensitive voices, those of Gustavo Adolfo Bécquer and Rosalía de Castro, remained apart from prevailing poetic tendencies. Their poetry, destined to be more enduring than that of their contemporaries, prolonged echoes of Romanticism and foreshadowed the spiritual and esthetic renovations of the succeeding movements.

Toward the turn of the century, a group of writers born in the 1860s and 1870s was coming of literary age. These writers were to become known as the Generation of 1898; their contemporaries in Spanish America were known as the Modernists. These movements of the Hispanic world—or, as some critics consider them, parallel aspects of a single movement—represented a reaction, in turn, to Realism. Objectivity, determinism, fascination with the tangible and material, and enthusiasm for scientific and social progress were supplanted by a new subjectivity and concentration on the imaginative and the beautiful. The writers of the Generation of 1898 shared with the Modernists a concern for precision of style and renovation of language, a horror of middle class values, and a belief in the dignity and mission of art. In subject matter, they turned to the crisis of Spain and its spiritual identity and destiny. The study of these movements leads into the twentieth century, and yet does not lead away from the subject of Rosalía de Castro. This is where the most enduring part of her work truly belongs. She anticipated the spiritual anguish which was to beset the modern poets and thinkers and, a generation before, was groping for stylistic liberation which they were to effect. Among her closest soul-mates, aside from Bécquer, are the twentieth-century writers Unamuno, Azorín, Antonio Machado, and the Portuguese poet Fernando Pessoa.

CHAPTER 2

Galicia

ROSALÍA is so strongly identified with Galicia that its presence and influence in her life and works must be examined. Azorín (José Martínez Ruiz, 1873–1967), an eminent member of the Generation of 1898, has remarked: "Galicia and Rosalía de Castro . . . Upon putting the pen to the paper to inscribe the word 'Galicia,' already our spirit had evoked—with vivid, deep emotion—the image of Rosalía de Castro." (*"Galicia y Rosalía de Castro . . . Al poner la pluma en el papel para estampar la palabra 'Galicia,' ya nuestro espíritu había evocado—con viva, honda emoción—la figura de Rosalía de Castro."*)[1] This region of long literary tradition and strong local identity found its poet in a modest, sensitive woman imbued with the spirit of the land, its people, and its aspirations. It is characteristic of the Spaniard to have a strong sense of place and loyalty to the *patria chica* (little fatherland), and the Galician is particularly noted for his strong attachment to his land.

I *The Land*

Galicia occupies the remote northwest corner of the Iberian Peninsula, surrounded on two sides by the sea, bounded by Portugal to the south, and adjoining the rest of Spain in the highlands of Asturias and Leon. Its promontory Finisterre, which juts into the Atlantic on the westernmost part of the European continent, was regarded in ancient times as the edge of the world. Galicia is a land of varied geography—rugged coasts, majestic mountains, gentle valleys—its rocky ribs sheathed in abundant vegetation. The presence of water is everywhere in sea, estuaries, streams, rain, and mist.

19

II *History*

Throughout its early history, Galicia was occupied and settled by a series of peoples, including Suabians, Iberians, and Celts. The name Galicia derives from the Roman designation *Calaicia,* "Land of the Celts." Ruins remain of structures and sites of these ancient inhabitants, and a more subtle residue persists in language, customs, and beliefs. Roman relics abound—bridges, fortifications, shrines, as well as the Roman legacy of language, culture, and institutions common to all areas once part of the Roman world. The Moors also penetrated the northwest corner of the peninsula, but their influence was not so prolonged there as in the south. They seem to have left a lasting impression in the minds of the folk, however, for many legends are linked to them, and in Galicia archaeological ruins, whatever the origin, may be referred to as *"coisas dos moros"* (Moorish things).

Christianity became deeply rooted in Galicia. One of the most famous of medieval shrines was there, at Santiago de Compostela. According to legend, the intact body of St. James the Apostle was discovered in the place now known as Compostela in the year 812 or 813. Supposedly the remains had been brought to the shores of Galicia around 44 A.D., after St. James had been martyred in Jerusalem. A pagan queen, after her conversion, allowed the body to be buried. Centuries later a hermit, led by a bright star, discovered the grave.[2] St. James or Santiago became the patron saint of the Spaniards, inspiring and protecting them against the Moors. The place where his body was found was considered the most holy spot in Spain and one of the three most holy in Christendom, ranking with Jerusalem and Rome.

Compostela was reached by the rest of Europe through France, along the famous Route of Santiago. Pilgrims of all categories traveled the road. Those hardy enough to survive the rugged mountain passes and other hazards of the journey thronged the streets of Santiago de Compostela. The city became a great cultural center as well as a religious one. The influence of French poetry, particularly of the refined school of Provence, mingled with the Spanish and the indigenous Galician poetry to give Santiago one of the most admired literatures of the medieval peninsula. The impressive cathedral which stands there today dates from the eleventh century, earlier structures having been destroyed by the Muslims. An eighteenth-century façade was the last major addition. This cathedral with its powerful aura affects all Galicians; it is a strong presence in Rosalía's works.

When the political center of Spain shifted to Castile and central Spain around the fifteenth century, Galicia was left on the fringes. It had not been part of Portugal since the twelfth century, and was thus isolated by the national boundary from its cultural and spiritual sibling. Hence Galicia has remained something of a stranger to both Iberian nations. Industry, communications, and transportation of recent times have changed this somewhat, yet twentieth-century accounts indicate that the isolation and persistence of the past are still a reality.[3]

III   *The People*

The social make-up of Galicia in the nineteenth century included the old aristocracy on their immense country estates; an urban middle class in the thriving port cities; and wealthy "americanos," the fortunate who returned rich from America. The middle class and the newly rich bought their social status and were influenced by the manners of Madrid and foreign capitals such as Paris. Then as today, however, society was largely composed of the common laboring folk—farmers and fishermen. Although Rosalía descended from an aristocratic family and lived a middle class life as the wife of a historian and bureaucrat, her sympathy was with the simple folk, their everyday concerns and traditional beliefs. It is the folk who give the individual stamp to regional characteristics, so that in speaking of Galician traits, it is this group which will be discussed. The spirit of the folk belongs to everyone and pervades all levels of life, appearing in the works of the most cosmopolitan and sophisticated writers. Rosalía's typically Galician compositions evoked recognition from everyone familiar with and loyal to Galicia.

Much of what might be said with regard to the condition and character of the Galician people of Rosalía's century still applies in our own. The farmers and fisherfolk have always been subject to poverty. Their small plot of earth is insufficient to meet the needs of the family, especially when subdivided among numerous descendents. The sea begrudgingly yields up its sustenance. The men have often been forced to emigrate to America or other parts of Spain or Europe, in search of survival if not of fortune. The women have assumed tasks and responsibilities which would have been the masculine role, and have developed the hardy qualities dictated by necessity, though always retaining the gentle characteristics of affection and sentiment. It has been their lot through the ages to look out to sea, waiting for their sons, husbands, fathers, or lovers. To the Galician, the sea has always meant separation and death rather than conquest or adventure.

The Galician peasant is still known for his industriousness and practicality. In America he has proved himself a hardworking, successful colonist, though his sentiments remain in the homeland. In the rest of Spain, Galicia has been regarded as out-of-the-way and backward, and the Galician as rustic and uncouth. He is often the target of jokes and his strange accent is mocked. The Galician, in turn, may react to this prejudice with scorn for other Spaniards and an exaggerated attachment to his region.

Isolation and strong ethnic identification have contributed to the preservation of traditional customs and beliefs. The Galician, now as in Rosalía's times, is very close to nature, associating it with mysterious supernatural powers. Invisible beings inhabit the forests— witches (*meigas, lurpias*) and elves (*trasgos*). The Host of Souls in Torment (*a compaña*) may beset and terrify, or carry away, the unwary nocturnal traveler. The word for hearth is *lar*, after the Roman familiar deities, the *lares*, and the fire is considered sacred. Myths, superstitions, folk medicine, and magic rites of ancient origin persist, now fused and confused with elements of Christianity. The revered cults of saints and feast days incorporate pagan rituals, as the sacred sites mark the locations of prehistoric shrines. In the words of the Galician author Ramón del Valle-Inclán (1866–1936): "Santiago of Galicia has been one of the sanctuaries of the world, and the souls there still keep their eyes intent upon the miracle! . . ." ("*¡Santiago de Galicia ha sido uno de los santuarios del mundo, y las almas todavía guardan allí los ojos atentos para el milagro! . . .*")[4]

IV *Literary Heritage*

Galicia has had a long and illustrious literary heritage. No one really knows how long, for its origins are lost in the mist of remote oral tradition. Its earliest written lyrics are among the oldest on the peninsula. The discovery of the *jarchas* (refrains in primitive Romance, transliterated in Arabic or Hebrew characters and dating from the mid-ninth century) in 1948 gave Andalucía the claim to the

oldest known lyrics in a Romance language in Spain. It is reasonable
to conjecture, however, that similar lyrics existed in Galicia as well
as in other parts of the peninsula in very early times, but did not
happen to be preserved in writing. The earliest written Galician-
Portuguese lyrics date from the late twelfth century and no doubt
had undergone a long period of oral development before being incorporated into more erudite written compositions. The oral tradition has flowed without interruption in the lore of the folk, and
echoes of it still persist.

Written literature begins with the medieval *cancioneiros* (collections of songs) in Galician-Portuguese. These reflect the thriving
school of poetry which had developed in Santiago de Compostela,
holy shrine of St. James and teeming crossroads of medieval culture,
where the poets or troubadours of Spain were in contact with European artistiç currents, especially the Provençal movement in southern France. Galician-Portuguese was refined and elevated as the
poetic medium of the peninsula, the preferred language for lyrics, a
position it retained until the fifteenth century. King Alfonso X, "The
Wise," of Castile and Leon (1221–1284), patron of learning and
letters and noted medieval figure who gave great impetus to the use
of Castilian as a language of prose, wrote his poetic works, the
Cantigas de Santa Maria (Canticles of Holy Mary), and other compositions in Galician-Portuguese.

The poetry of the Galician-Portuguese troubadours has come
down to us in three *cancioneiros:* the *Cancioneiro da Ajuda*,
thought to have been collected in the Portuguese court at the end of
the thirteenth century and discovered in the monastery of Ajuda in
Portugal; the *Cancioneiro da Biblioteca Nacional*, kept in the National Library of Portugal and sometimes referred to as *Cancioneiro
Colluci-Brancuti* after two Italian scholars who had possessed it; and
the *Cancioneiro da Vaticana*, which is also a copy made in Italy and
found in the Vatican Library. The copies found in Italy were produced in the sixteenth century from fourteenth-century originals.
These collections of songs contain over two thousand poems by
some two hundred different poets, including King Alfonso X and
King Dinis of Portugal.[5]

The poems found in these collections are of three types: *cantigas
d'amor* (songs of love); *cantigas d'amigo* (songs to the friend or
lover); and *cantigas d'escárnio* (satirical songs). The *cantigas d'amor*
are strongly influenced by the Provençal courtly love tradition—

ingenious and conventional tributes of the enamoured troubadour to his haughty lady. The *cantigas d'amigo* are laments of a girl for her absent lover and are simpler and more natural, closer to the indigenous tradition. The *cantigas d'escárnio* are clever and humorous verbal insults, often directed to real people. Although couched in the elegant, courtly forms, they employ insinuating plays on words and, at times, coarse allusions.[6]

By the time of the Marqués de Santillana (1398–1458), Castilian had become dominant as the literary language in Spain, and Portuguese was developing independently. The Galician language endured, largely in unwritten form, as the everyday language of the region, until its literary revival in the nineteenth century. Down through the centuries, however, Galicians have figured prominently in Spanish literature. As examples, one has only to recall such eminent writers as Benito Jerónimo Feijoo, Emilia Pardo Bazán, and Ramón del Valle-Inclán, among a host of others.

V   *Cultural Revival*

In the early part of the nineteenth century there occurred in Galicia a resurgence of local patriotism, the outgrowth of Romanticism and of political conditions in Spain. Similar movements arose in other culturally distinct regions of Spain, such as Catalonia and the Basque Provinces. France also experienced this phenomenon in such areas as Provence and Brittany. The Galician Restoration was both political and cultural in nature. The language became the rallying point of the regional enthusiasts, who proposed to revive the idiom as artistic medium and to cultivate an authentic literary expression. Political issues included the desire for recognition of cultural individuality and protest against the increasing centralization of the national government, with the consequent neglect of regional problems. The movement's "patriarch," Manuel Murguía (Rosalía's husband), and other leaders sought to create a Galician consciousness. To enhance their unique heritage and differentiation from the rest of Spain, they emphasized their Celtic nature, fusing history and myth, and stressed their resemblance to Portugal. As Murguía maintained, "its language is as much ours as its seas."[7] The folk tradition was also avidly exploited.

The leaders of the Restoration were a group of intense intellectuals and political activists which included Nicomedes Pastor Díaz, Enrique Pondal, Manuel Curros, Aurelio Aguirre, and Manuel

Murguía. Rosalía, with her deep empathy for the folk, her absorption of their themes and art forms, and her lyric talent, was instrumental in the movement as exponent of Galician character and life and as renovator of the language. The political fervor spent itself, but the cultural revival made lasting contributions. Studies of Galician language and culture and literary works in Galician continue to be produced by scholars and writers of the region.[8]

The language that nineteenth-century writers undertook to utilize for their literary efforts had suffered some five centuries of erosion and neglect. It had survived in home and marketplace in an untutored, oral state, full of inconsistencies and incorrections, vulnerable to influences from the official language, Castilian. Each writer transliterated it as he would from his own experience, reflecting sub-regional variations as well as individual interpretations. Grammars and dictionaries were compiled to enforce some order on the chaos. Rosalía's particular variety represents the region of Santiago de Compostela, but she was little concerned with consistency and standardization. She proceeded spontaneously, reproducing the cadences by ear, much as a folk singer might reproduce his songs without consulting a musical score. Variations in spelling, verb endings, and pronoun forms are, in Rosalía's production, artistically enriching, allowing flexibility to fit demands of meter or rhyme.

CHAPTER 3

Biography

I *Early Life*

ROSALÍA de Castro's birth was registered in the Hospital Real of Santiago de Compostela on February 24, 1837. This is generally accepted as the date of her birth. Somewhat mysterious circumstances surround the first days of her life. The infant was brought to be registered and baptised by a woman called María Francisca Martínez, a servant of the mother's family, who acted as godmother and did not enter the child in the foundling asylum. The child was christened María Rosalía Rita, "of unknown parentage."[1]

Rosalía's mother was María Teresa da Cruz de Castro y Abadía, daughter of an old and noble Galician family of Padrón (also called Iria Flavia), near Santiago. Her father has been identified as José Martínez Viojo, a seminarian who later served as priest in Padrón. The mother did not immediately assume care of the child, and Rosalía grew up in the country on the estate "La Mahía" at Castro Ortuño, near Santiago.[2] Somewhere between the ages of ten and thirteen she went to live with her mother in Santiago. Even though Rosalía did not live with her mother during her early childhood, there was a close bond of affection between them. The extent of Rosalía's acquaintance with her father is uncertain.

Little is known of Rosalía's early years. The child no doubt loved and absorbed the sights and sounds of nature in her rural environment, and there she learned the songs and lore of the Galician people. In Santiago, after joining her mother, her formal education took place. She attended school at the Sociedad Económica de Amigos del País (Association of Friends of the Country) and received what was then considered suitable instruction for a well-bred young lady. Her accomplishments included music (guitar), drawing, and French. She took part in the literary and cultural activities of Santiago and attended the Liceo de la Juventud (Lyceum for Youth)

26

held in the convent of San Agustín. The Lyceum, one of the many such groups founded in Spain during the Romantic era, was a cultural association which provided a meeting place for writers and artists. There Rosalía mingled with regional intellectual figures.

Her talents for music, writing, and the theater became evident early in her life. She is said to have begun composing verses at the age of eleven or twelve and she took part in the Lyceum's dramatic productions. Her literary formation took place during Spanish Romanticism, which had been fed by the English, French, and German. Rosalía read French and knew other foreign authors through French or Spanish translations. She undoubtedly read extensively in the Spanish classics, and perhaps knew some Portuguese masterpieces as well. The youthful period spent in Santiago would correspond almost exactly with the intense social, intellectual, and artistic activities of the Galician Restoration.

In 1856 Rosalía went to Madrid, where she stayed with a relative of her mother's, Carmen Lugín de Castro.[3] There in "The Court," as Madrid was called (this was during the reign of Isabel II), the young girl was exposed to theatrical productions and literary events of the time and had access to poetry, fiction, and reviews published in periodicals such as *La Iberia* and *El Museo Universal*. Too shy to attend the fashionable salons to which she was invited, Rosalía may have met some of the young writers, among them Valeriano and Gustavo Adolfo Bécquer and perhaps Manuel Murguía, in more intimate gatherings or *tertulias* held in Doña Carmen's home. All the while, Rosalía was quietly writing. In 1857 her first collection of poems appeared, a slender volume entitled *La flor (The Flower)*. The book was favorably reviewed by Murguía in *La Iberia*.[4] He claimed not to know the author, although he almost certainly had known her previously in Santiago, as well as in Madrid. In any event, Rosalía and Manuel Murguía were engaged that same year and were married in Madrid on October 10, 1858.

II *Marriage, Family, Literary Activities*

The man Rosalía married, Manuel Martínez Murguía, was a Galician of Basque descent, born in San Tirso de Oleiros, in the province of La Coruña, in 1833. He studied pharmacy, but followed the careers of journalist and historian. He was a writer of some note, author of several novels and a number of books of historical and literary content.[5] He is honored in Galicia as "Patriarch of Galician letters" because of his role as promotor and leader of the Galician regionalist movement. His career included a number of responsible and prestigious positions: director of the periodical *La Oliva* in Vigo, Government Historian (Jefe del Archivo) in Simancas, head of the Regional Archives of Galicia in La Coruña, director of the Archives and Library of the University of Santiago, and editor of the periodical *La Ilustración Gallega y Asturiana* in Madrid. He encouraged and supported his wife's literary efforts and left a number of accounts and documents concerning her life and works.

It is difficult to determine with any degree of accuracy what Manuel Murguía was really like as a person. References to him are sometimes unflattering. As a creative writer he was indeed less spectacular than his wife, but, realizing this, he encouraged her and made no effort to suppress her talents. In physical appearance, he was evidently small of stature and slightly built, and he is sometimes referred to as a "dwarf." A photograph of the Murguía family shows him to be normal in appearance and proportion, although there is no way to determine his relative height from the arrangement of the figures in the picture.[6] From all indications, he was an intelligent, energetic, and talented man, competent in his chosen fields. He survived Rosalía by thirty-eight years and died in 1923 at the age of ninety.

After their marriage, the Murguías returned to Santiago. There a daughter, Alejandra, was born in 1859. That same year, Rosalía's first novel, *La hija del mar (Child from the Sea)*, was published. A second novel, *Flavio*, appeared in 1861. The death of Rosalía's beloved mother, Doña Teresa de Castro, occurred in 1862. A brief volume of poems entitled *A mi madre (To My Mother)* was published in a small private edition in 1863. The year 1863 also saw the appearance of Rosalía's first major work and her triumph as a writer, with the publication of *Cantares gallegos (Galician songs)*. Murguía recounts its inception in *Los precursores (The Precursors)*. During one of the sojourns in central Spain (Simancas) in 1861, Rosalía was consumed with nostalgia for her homeland. As a tribute to Galicia and an outlet for her emotions, she began to write a poem inspired by a familiar Galician refrain, *"Adiós, rios, adiós, fontes"* ("Farewell, rivers, farewell, springs").[7] This poem, submitted by Murguía without Rosalía's knowledge, was published in *El Museo Universal*, September 24, 1861. Murguía then urged her to write for publication more poems based on popular lyrics. She did so, rapidly and easily, recalling a familiar couplet and embellishing it with her own personal variations. She was reluctant to publish them, however, wishing them to appear as Murguía's. Finally she agreed to release the compositions in her own name. *Cantares gallegos (Galician songs)* was an immediate success, especially in Galicia.

A series of prose works followed: *Ruinas (Ruins)*, a novelette, 1866; *"El cadiceño" ("The Man from Cádiz")*, a short story which appeared in *Almanaque de Galicia,* 1866; and *El caballero de las botas azules (The Gentleman of the Blue Boots)*, a novel, 1867. The Murguía's second child, another daughter, Aura, was born in Santiago in 1869. The following year, during another stay in Simancas, Rosalía began a series of poems which would constitute her second volume of poetry in Galician, *Follas novas (New Leaves)*. Like *Cantares gallegos*, it was "written in the desert of Castile," as the prologue reads. Because of the enthusiastic acceptance of *Cantares gallegos*, she felt a "debt of loyalty" to produce another, and final, tribute to the Galician people in their language. The composition of this book was to continue for the following ten years.

After 1871 the family resided in various places in Galicia. Twins, Gala and Ovidio, were born in 1871 or 1872 in Lestrove (province of La Coruña), and a daughter, Amara, in 1874, in La Coruña. A son, Adriano Honorato Alejandro, born in Santiago in 1875, died as the result of a fall before reaching the age of two. The last child, Valentina, born in Santiago in 1877, died at birth.[8]

From 1879 to 1882, Murguía was director of the periodical *La Ilustración Gallega y Asturiana* in Madrid. Rosalía remained in Lestrove with the children. Her second collection of poetry, *Follas novas (New Leaves)*, was published in 1880, after ten years in writing. A novel, *El primer loco (The First Madman)*, came out in 1881. Rosalía's final residence was at the estate called "La Matanza," near Padrón, where she completed the last collection of poetry and her last published book, *En las orillas del Sar (On the Banks of the River Sar)*, 1884.[9]

III *Final Days*

Rosalía died at noon on July 15, 1885, at "La Matanza." Ill health and physical suffering had beset her throughout her life. During her last few years she was slowly consumed by cancer of the uterus, in a time when there was no recourse to surgery or other treatments. She was aware of her irrevocable fate, a substantiation of all her premonitions of an early death. Her later writings and the final book, *En las orillas del Sar (On the Banks of the River Sar)*, are permeated with this awareness, expressed in terms of the human dilemma of love for life and knowledge of mortality. Dying slowly and painfully, writing almost up to the end, her exceptional mind lucid and her sensitive heart without bitterness, she left in these subdued yet intense poems a beautiful and moving statement of the "tragic sense of life."

Rosalía's death is poignantly related by Victoriano García Martí in his study *"Rosalía de Castro o el dolor de vivir"* ("Rosalía de Castro or the Sorrow of Life"), which prefaces his edition of her *Obras completas (Complete Works)*.[10] She asked to be buried in the cemetery of Andina, near her house. Her last words reportedly were: "Open that window, for I want to see the sea."[11] The sea was not visible from the house, but she had made a trip to the shore at the port of Carril shortly before she died. In 1891, the remains of Rosalía were exhumed and transferred, with great ceremony, to the Chapel of the Visitation in the Convent of Santo Domingo de Bonaval in Santiago, where they lie in a dignified marble tomb. As becomes a legend and a saint, the document of exhumation relates that her body was "scarcely disfigured," and that a bouquet of pansies on her breast, loving tribute of her eldest daughter, Alejandra, was only "slightly faded, as though recently cut."[12]

IV *The Person and the Writer*

Over the skeleton of chronological data, the biographer seeks to paint in the features, awaken the personality, and reconstruct the thoughts and feelings of the subject. In the case of Rosalía, even the factual material is none too certain. She left no diary, and only a few fragments of personal letters have survived. Some of her prologues and articles and a great many of the poems are personal in tone, but confessions which might be contained therein are filtered through the screen of literature. Murguía wrote a great deal about his wife, in loving and laudatory terms. These accounts, however, intended for the public eye and couched in florid literary style, cannot be taken as intimate revelations.

An aura of myth soon began to surround the poet, and many of the early biographical studies are idealized and sentimental. Later scholarship has probed and psychoanalyzed. Since one of Rosalía's unquestionable traits was modesty, all this curiosity and praise would have embarrassed her—and at times, perhaps, made her chuckle.

The very dearth of personal documents and mementos attests to this modesty. She had no notion that anyone would preoccupy himself with her life, nor would she have sought this attention, whatever ambitions she might have had for her works. The acclaim accorded to *Cantares gallegos* seemed to overwhelm her, but never went to her head, and there is no indication that she wished to be great or famous. Her Galician works reveal a sense of mission to defend and divulge the beauties of her land and to record the saga of its unsung heroes and heroines. She wrote as a writer must, because the passion of creativity could not be quenched. Her writings gave expression to an abundance of ideas and served to unburden her troubled soul.

Rosalía's works are indeed autobiographical, woven out of her experiences, both personal and vicarious. They reflect the preoccupations and themes which obsessed her and the human dramas which most affected her. They reveal an inner biography, wherein her observations, sensations, emotions, and literary influences are mingled, charged with imagination and fantasy. The connection between art and events is elusive, altered by artistic transformation and expressed indirectly through images, dramatic characters, and symbols. Great caution must be exercised in linking allusions in the poems or novels to specific occurrences in her life, at the risk of twisting the one or the other to make it fit, or of indulging in sheer conjecture. Rosalía had to an unusual degree the capacity to empathize—to absorb into herself the experiences of others, and to project herself into other identities. She expresses this tendency in the prologue to *Follas novas:* "Therefore I am not certain what there is in my book of my own griefs, or of those of others, although well I might consider them all as mine, for those accustomed to misfortune, come to count as their own those troubles which afflict others." (*"Por eso iñoro ó que haxa n' ò meu libro d' os propios pesares, ou d' os alleos, anque ben podo telos todos por meus, pois os acostumados â desgracia, chegan a contar por suas as que afrixen ôs demáis."*)[13]

It is possible to ascertain something of Rosalía's physical appearance. Several photographs and portraits exist.[14] A charming verbal description is given by her biographer Augusto González Besada, which bears resemblance to the portraits:

She was, according to contemporary accounts, tall and slender, with a faultless, light brunette complexion, deep black eyes and extremely thick black hair. Her mouth was quite large, with very red lips and perfect teeth, her nose short and well delineated, the oval shape of her face somewhat imperfect because of the prominent cheekbones. [She had] a prominent bust, narrow waist and finely shaped hands with very slender fingers. In repose, her expression was melancholic; but when she spoke, her eyelids fluttered and the eyes took on a singular beauty, as though they became larger because of the thick, curling lashes and the bright white of the eye which contrasted luminously against the deep blackness of the iris. Elegant of bearing, naturally graceful and light of movement, endowed with a lovely, sweet contralto voice, her outstanding attributes, more than beauty, were the interesting and mysterious quality of her features, the affability and simplicity of her manner and her love for music, birds and flowers.[15]

González Besada goes on to remark that later in life this description would not have resembled her, as she was emaciated and disfigured by her illness. Still that "sweet radiance of those eyes, windows to her sorrow-laden soul . . ." ("los dulces resplandores de aquellos ojos, a los que se asomaba el alma, transida de amarguras . . .") continued to soften and animate her face.[16]

The statue on the monument to her honor in Santiago (1917) portrays the Rosalía of early maturity and is faithful to the portraits and descriptions. The figure is seated in a calm, pensive attitude, and projects an aura of strength, gentleness, and warmth.

Certain traits of Rosalía's personality can be ascertained from statements made by others, her own personal remarks, and revelations of the works themselves. She was simple and modest in tastes and behavior, generous, loving, extremely sensitive and introspective, and often subject to melancholy. Her intelligence, courage, and integrity are evident. The impression of the sad, meditative person, though characteristic, is not wholly accurate, for she was capable of gaiety and humor as well.

The intimate details of her life are much more obscure. Some think she had an unhappy love affair as a young girl. Her early poems of La flor might seem to refer to such an experience. It is stated frequently that her marriage to Murguía was turbulent. Their private life remains curtained behind the velvet draperies of nineteenth-century propriety—an effective screen, though tongues may wag. She was a devoted wife and mother, taking this role as her first duty and best reward, and not considering it incompatible with writing. Nothing in the writings of either spouse would indicate undue friction or bitterness. Their intellectual interests were compatible and they collaborated in their literary efforts. Murguía's references to his wife in articles, prologues, and dedications are admiring and devoted, and she also speaks fondly of him in such documents. In the few letters from Rosalía to her husband which have been preserved, where real and intimate feelings are more likely to be exposed, the sentiments are affectionate. She protests that he does not write, expresses loneliness in his absence, and murmurs wifely confidences. The tone and content of these messages would indicate a close and loving relationship. There were no doubt some situational difficulties in the marriage—Murguía's absences because of his work and occasional financial straits. Rosalía's constant series of illnesses, and the losses of their young children, Adriano and Valentina, undoubtedly added hardship and grief to their lives.

The theme of *dolor*—which includes the various meanings of pain, suffering, and sorrow—is always associated with Rosalía's life and works. There is ample evidence of physical suffering in her life; she also had her share of personal sorrow and grief and was deeply affected by the sufferings of others. The *dolor* which pervades her work, however, transcends earthly causes and acquires metaphysical significance.

V *A Woman in Her Times*

The pronounced feminine quality of Rosalía's work has often been noted, and the gentle, maternal aspects of it stressed. She is indeed a feminine writer, avowedly but not apologetically so. She gives exquisite expression to certain identifiably feminine themes, such as the sorrow and heroism of Galician women and the joys and torments of love from the woman's point of view. Her work could never be called "effeminate," however, for even in her most immature efforts there is an underlying strength and artistry which remove it from the merely pretty or sentimental.

Some aspects of her work might be said to be "feminist." This retiring and soulful woman, best known for her enduring and universal poetry, was also very much in touch with her own times and aroused by social injustices, particularly those which affected women. She did not rebel against her traditional home and family role nor seek legal or political equality. There is one point upon which she did take issue—intellectual and artistic liberation. She was not unique in her perception of this question, for the latter half of the nineteenth century in Spain saw the triumph of a number of significant women writers, such as Cecilia Bohl de Faber [Fernán Caballero], Concepción Arenal, Gertrudis Gómez de Avellaneda, and Emilia Pardo Bazán. The theme of the position and education of women was widely treated in the novels of the time, and some of the strongest and most penetrating statements were made by men, notably Benito Pérez Galdós and Leopoldo Alas [Clarín]. When a woman picked up a pen, the outraged cry *"una mujer literata"* ("a literary woman") went up from society to thwart and humiliate her.

Rosalía made a number of references to this attitude, some with a definitely bitter edge. For a woman of her day, she was fortunate with regard to her own intellectual and literary outlets. She had never been denied the right to read and to express herself. She wrote freely, with the approval of her husband, as well as the praise of the educated public and receptivity of the publishers. She never adopted a masculine pen name, and was generally known simply as Rosalía de Castro.[17] There are indications, however, that she felt the disapproval of provincial society, which thought her presumptuous and eccentric, and perhaps of her mother's genteel relatives. Her protests were not motivated by purely personal resentments, but espoused the cause of sisters less free than herself, trapped by notions of respectability and social status, or by poverty and ignorance.

Rosalía faced (and coped with) the dilemma of the intelligent and creative woman in a closed, intolerant society in an honest and courageous way. She did not seek to enter or compete in a masculine world or to enhance women at the expense of men. Above all, she did not pretend to be what she was not or to tread men's footsteps simply because they seemed to have the advantage. For her, femininity, with its attributes of imagination, sentiment, compassion, and intuition, was a source of creativity and an access to poetry. She wrestled with the comprehension and expression of the essence of life with the particular sensibilities she possessed. Men per se were not the enemy; her own sex came in for its share of criticism. Rosalía's rebellion was against injustice, oppression, hypocrisy, prejudice, and mediocrity wherever they might exist.

CHAPTER 4

Early Poetry

I La flor (The Flower)

ROSALÍA'S first published work, a slender volume of poetry entitled *La flor*, appeared in Madrid in 1857. The book, as well as its author, attracted the attention of the young Galician journalist, Manuel Murguía, who gave it recognition in an article, *"La flor, poesías de la señorita Rosalía de Castro"* (*"The Flower*, poems by Miss Rosalía de Castro"), published in *La Iberia*, May 12, 1857. In the article he remarked on her talent and urged her to continue to cultivate poetry. He confessed that her verses had moved him deeply, commended her frank expression of sentiments, and noted that Espronceda was apparently her teacher. Perhaps, he ventured, the young poetess "was born to be something more than a woman, perhaps to bestow an honorable name to her country" (*"ha nacido para ser algo más que una mujer, tal vez para legar un nombre honroso a su patria"*).[1] Although he disclaimed acquaintance with the author of *La flor*, this is debatable, since they were both from Santiago, had been associated with the Lyceum there, and announced their engagement soon after the appearance of the article.

La flor is a brief collection containing six rather long, rambling poems in which, as Murguía noticed, the debt to Romantic models, especially Espronceda and Zorrilla, is manifest. Several of the poems employ the narrative-dramatic form so favored by the Romantics to recreate legends or personal fantasies. The use of a variety of meters which pulsate with the emotional tempo of theme or narrative is another Romantic technique. The rhyme is consonant, in varying patterns; the tone overwrought and desperate. The settings are often conventionally Romantic—dark windy nights in cemeteries or a backdrop of nature in melancholy moods. The vocabulary tends toward hyperbolic terms, such as "fatidic" and "tetric."

35

The themes which predominate in *La flor* are impossible and tragic love with its ensuing disillusionment and despair, loss of innocence and faith, unfortunate destiny, hostility and sarcasm on the part of society, and longing for solitude and death. The "flower" of the title is a recurrent motif and suggests a number of interpretations: life, youth, illusions, innocence, purity, and love. It is associated with fleeting pleasures and fond hopes soon withered by the storms and winds of adversity, leaving the poet in a solitary desert, where nothingness looms: "Because once that flower of my gardens was dead,/ nothingness . . . , all has turned to nothingness." (*"Porque esa flor de mis jardines muerta,/ nada . . ., en nada no más se ha convertido."* 222).[2] All of the poems, and particularly the intensely personal "Fragmentos" ("Fragments"), refer to a grievous disenchantment with life and a shattering crisis of faith which leaves the poet in utter despair: "I was alone with my unfathomable grief/ in the abyss of an imbecile world!" (*"¡Sola era yo con mi dolor profundo/ en el abismo de un imbécil mundo!"* 219).

Although the style is unformed, the sentiments over-emoted, and many of the ideas and expressions familiar Romantic commonplaces, the poems of *La flor* are not trite and vacuous. They cannot be dismissed as a precocious tour de force or mere pastiche of Romantic influences. The reader is struck by the emotional intensity and depth of comprehension of this young woman. The content might be attributed, on the one hand, to the assimilation of Romantic modes, wherein youths of twenty summers sing of the "autumn" of life and prepare to hurl themselves into the abyss of nothingness because of disappointed love or lost illusions. On the other hand, it might reflect the predilections of an impressionable girl for the dramatic and tragic. Nonetheless, much of Rosalía herself and a kernel of lived experience can be sensed. It is possible that the poems refer to an unhappy amorous experience of her own. The betrayal and abandonment of her mother, which Rosalía must have felt deeply, would also have given her insight into the pleasures and deceptions of love. Most of the poems are stated in the first person, using fictitious feminine personages—Argelina and Inés—which might be taken as masks for herself or her mother. The full extent of confessional material in the book is impossible to determine, although it is definitely personal in tone. Its significance in Rosalía's total poetic development is indisputable. To trace the trajectory of a writer, it is necessary to read backwards, in search of roots and seeds. Already present in this first, immature effort are the dark themes of nothingness, death, solitude, sorrow, rejection by society, and religious doubt. Some of the images used to convey these themes will characterize her later works: the shadow or phantom, fallen tree of faith, sea of sorrows, withered flower of hope, abyss of nothingness, thorns, desert, weary journey. The germs of Rosalía's deepest poetry can be found here; she has already begun to select from her literary and vital experience the meaningful elements. The anguished subjectivity of *La flor* will culminate in *Follas novas (New Leaves)* and *En las orillas del Sar (On the Banks of the River Sar)*.

II   A mi madre (To My Mother)

In the interval between the publication of *La flor* (1857) and 1863, Rosalía married Manuel Murguía in 1858, bore her first child, Alejandra in 1859, and published two novels: *La hija del mar (Child from the Sea)* in 1859 and *Flavio* in 1861. The death of her beloved mother, Doña Teresa de Castro y Abadía, in 1862 occasioned the publication of a small private edition of poems the following year. The poems are, as could be expected, emotional and elegiac, with a personal intensity lent by the immediate experience with grief and Rosalía's deep affection for her mother. Thematically, the poet progresses from personal, specific sentiments to meditations on the universal experience of death, sorrow, brevity of life, abandonment, and desolation. Her grief is embittered by feelings of remorse for her ingratitude and failure to fully appreciate her mother's love and suffering in life. Although the poems are of limited literary importance, they reveal the characteristic tendency of Rosalía to release her intimate feelings through lyrical outlets.

CHAPTER 5

Cantares gallegos (Galician Songs)

I *Background*

THE year 1863 saw the appearance of Rosalía's first important book, *Cantares gallegos*. This collection of poems inspired by the poetry, songs, dances, and folklore of Galicia was to bring her lasting recognition. Local customs and popular lore had fascinated scholars and writers since the *costumbrismo* enthusiasm of the Romantic period, and this early interest in the peculiar cultural manifestations of the various regions had accomodated itself to the trend toward Realism in the latter half of the century.

In Galicia, writers fired with patriotic fervor had turned their pens into weapons to revive, enhance, and defend their unique culture, and to foment their political aspirations. Since early in the century efforts had been made to create a Galician consciousness, combining history, folklore, and the resurrection of the language. A fever of journalistic and literary activity produced compositions on Galician subjects, many of which were written in Galician. Rosalía's predecessors who enjoyed a certain renown in their time include Nicomedes Pastor Díaz, Juan Manuel Pintos, Francisco Añón, and Alberto Camino. Her contemporaries in the group associated with the Lyceum of Youth in Santiago include Aurelio Aguirre, Manuel Murguía, and Enrique Pondal. A younger contemporary of merit was Manuel Curros Enríquez. These writers were not of the folk, but sought in the folk and in their language and traditions the authentic identity of the region and evidence of its differentiation from other regions of Spain. Theirs was an erudite and artificial recreation, "the popular soul contemplated and configurated by those who are not folk." ("*alma popular contemplada y configurada por quienes no son pueblo.*")[1]

Of all the regional group, Rosalía is the only one who would be familiar to anyone but the literary historian or Galician specialist, and of all the poems produced in that vein, hers must certainly stand out as the most memorable. In *Cantares*, the interpenetration of writer and folk is so nearly perfect that the esthetic distance is barely perceptible. She was a truly successful regionalist, in whose work her subjects could recognize themselves, and a wider audience could see and comprehend the Galicians, as well as respond to universal themes and sentiments. Rosalía did not aspire to become the idol of the Galician Restoration and had no political ambitions. Later remarks may indicate that she resented the adulation and felt exploited by the cause. Her songs originated as an outpouring of her own sentiments, and she intended them as a tribute to Galicia and a defense of her neglected and much maligned land.

II *Genesis, Intent, and Sources*

As mentioned in Chapter 3, Rosalía wrote the first poem of *Cantares* with no intention of compiling a book. While with Murguía in Simancas, suffering from acute homesickness, she recalled the popular Galician refrain "*Adiós, ríos, adiós, fontes*" ("Farewell, rivers, farewell, springs"), and elaborated upon it with variations of her own. At Murguía's insistence, she composed other poems in a similar manner. Hesitant at first, she finally agreed to release the collection for publication in her own name.

In the prologue, the author explains her intentions in writing the book and apologizes for her shortcomings as poet and interpreter of Galicia: "But no one is less endowed than I with the great qualities necessary to carry out such a difficult task, although no one could be moved by a greater desire to sing the beauties of our land in that soft and gentle dialect which those who do not know that it excels other languages in sweetness and harmony would call barbaric." (*"Mais naide ten menos qu'eu teño as grandes cualidades que son precisas prá levar a cabo obra tan difícile, anque naide tampouco se pudo achar animado d' un máis bon deseo prá cantar as bellezas da nosa terra n' aquel dialecto soave e mimoso que queren facer bárbaro os que non saben que aventaxa as demáis linguas en doçura e armonía."* 259). She states that her only school was that of "our poor country folk" (259), and pays tribute to a contemporary author, Antonio Trueba, whose *El libro de los cantares (The Book of Songs;* 1852), based on popular poetry, was her model and incentive. Rosalía greatly admired Trueba, and could not suspect that her own *Cantares* would far surpass those of her predecessor. She expresses the hope that her book will be an eloquent defense of Galicia against the unjust opinions held in the rest of Spain, particularly in Castile, so haughty, ugly, and desolate in Rosalía's mind. The principal source of *Cantares* is the rich lyrical and aphoristic lore of Galicia, which Rosalía had absorbed from the folk she knew intimately, such as her childhood nurse, "La Choina." She also knew and admired the works of other poets who had incorporated folk motifs into their poems—the above-mentioned Antonio Trueba, Ventura Ruiz Aguilera, and Augusto Ferrán, among others.

She does not set out to be a bard, as did Enrique Pondal, but rather a minstrel, personified in the "*meniña gaitera*" or bagpipe girl. Her songs are not grandly heroic; they attempt to recount the humble epic of simple people. Although accurately representing the people, *Cantares* is not just a collection of folk songs. The contribution of the poet is apparent throughout. It is theirs and hers. The subjective content is admitted by the author in the prologue, where she states that the songs were "gathered by my heart as my own heritage" ("*recollidos pó-lo meu coraçón como harencia propia*" 260). Her selection and interpretations are guided by her emotions and memory. The glosses or elaborations, while keeping to the theme and spirit of the refrain, allow her a certain artistic freedom. The perennial universality and freshness of the folk and the lyrical sensitivity of the author combine to make these poems accessible and moving to a far wider audience than a few regional enthusiasts. The volume is dedicated to Fernán Caballero, pioneer of the Spanish realistic novel, whom Rosalía admired as writer and interpreter of folk customs.

III   *Language*

Cantares gallegos is written in the Galician dialect most familiar to Rosalía, that spoken on the shores of the Sar River, around Santiago de Compostela, and in the Amabia and Ulla River regions. It is her second, or other, language, one with which she is comfortable, and the one in which the motifs which inspire her are couched. She uses the language natively and naturally, and writes it "by ear." There is a great deal of inconsistency in spelling and in vocabulary and verb forms, reflecting the vacillations which occur in the spoken language, owning to the fusion of the old Galician-Portuguese forms with elements absorbed from Castilian. The resulting fluctuation is characteristic of a language not systematized by written conventions and fragmented within itself into numerous sub-regional variants. Rosalía preserves the oral quality and turns the multiplicity of forms to artistic advantage, selecting the form which best suits her thought or line. Her use of diacritical marks, although inconsistent, represents an attempt to indicate pronunciation, contractions, and elisions, somewhat in the manner of modern Portuguese usage. Spelling and accents in the material quoted have been left as they appear in the edition cited.

A few observations on pronunciation and orthography may be of interest to those who wish to consult the Galician:

(1) The pronunciation corresponds approximately to Spanish (except for *x*, discussed below). Rosalía uses the *seseo*, and sometimes confuses *c* and *s* in spelling: *siudades* for *ciudades*, *seo* for ceo (i.e. *cielo*). *B* and *v* are pronounced identically and are also confused in spelling: *ban* for *van*, *vaixo* for *baixo* (Spanish *bajo*). Stress follows the Spanish pattern. (2) There are also a great many similarities to Portuguese. The *x* is pronounced as in Portuguese (English *sh*), and occurs where Castilian would have *ge*, *gi*, and *j*. The definite articles are *o*, *a*, *os*, *as*, and contractions occur between prepositions and articles: *pó-la* (Portuguese *pela;* Spanish *por la*); *do* (Spanish *del*); *á* (Spanish *a la*). Pronouns often follow verb forms: *olvídasme* instead of *me olvidas*. The article is often used with possessives: *a miña terra*. The sounds represented by *r* and *l* are frequently interchanged: *afrixir* (Spanish *aflijir*); *frol* (*flor*). *Ch* equals Spanish *ll*: *chove*; *chora*; *chama*; and *f* equals Spanish *h*: *fillo (hijo)*; *ferida* (*herida*). The diphthongization of *e* to *ie* and *o* to *ue* does not occur: *morte*; *fero*; however, the diphthongs *ei* and *ou*, characteristic of Portuguese, are found: *veiga; chouza*. The diminutive ending *-iño*, so favored in Portuguese (*-inho*), and occasionally used in Spanish, occurs with great frequency in Galician. (3) The vocabulary combines forms from both Spanish and Portuguese, with some variations peculiarly Galician: *che* for *te*; *ti* for Spanish *tú* or Portuguese *tu*; *cál* for Spanish *cual* or Portuguese *qual*.[2]

IV   *Organization and Forms*

The poems of *Cantares* are loosely organized within a "frame." The first and the final poems of the original edition (four more poems were added in later editions) are recited by a character called the *"Meniña gaitera"* or "lively bagpipe girl," who represents the author. (*Gaitero* can mean both "bagpipe player" or the gaiety and liveliness usually assocated with such music.) When asked to sing, the lass begins with a lively poem of introduction: "I shall sing for you, Galicia,/ your sweet songs . . ." (*"Cantart' ei, Galicia,/ teus doçes cantares . . ."* 268). In closing, at what was originally the end of the book, she modestly apologizes for her inadequate efforts, but says she did the best she could: "I did not express myself as I should like/ because I'm not very expressive;/ but though I lack talent/ I burst with love for my country . . ." (*"Non me expriquei cal quixera/ pois son de expricanza pouca;/ si gracia en cantar non teño/ o amor da pátria m' afoga . . ."* 376).

Each poem incorporates in some way a popular motif. The usual pattern is to begin with a quote from the folk repertoire, which is followed by an original variation or gloss. This may be a little story or drama or may contain personal reflections. The poetic forms come, for the most part, from the popular tradition, and have had a long and pervasive influence on the poetry of the Iberian Peninsula. They are singable, danceable cadences which adapt to—or derive from—the language itself. The resemblance they bear to the medieval poetry which has been preserved is not coincidental. The medieval *cancioneiros* were not known in Rosalía's day,[3] but the living tradition of the *cantigas d'amigo* (songs to the friend or lover), and the festive rounds and dances which inspired the medieval poets, have come down through the centuries in the songs and lore of the folk. A recently issued recording of Spanish folk music includes two songs from Galicia which contain refrains Rosalía used: *"Adiós, ríos . . ."* ("Farewell, rivers . . .") and *"Fun ô muiño . . ."* ("I went to the mill . . .").[4]

The line may be based on accentual rhythms, corresponding to the beats of choral singing or dance steps, or on syllable count (as literary poetry is measured). Some of the most typical metric forms used in *Cantares* will be discussed briefly.

The *gaita gallega,* or Galician bagpipe song, has a varying number of syllables, usually ten or eleven, with four strong beats per line (it may also be written in shorter lines of two strong beats each). It is a lively, light-hearted cadence, sung to triple 6/8 musical accompaniment. This form is also known as the *muiñeira* (mill song), perhaps deriving from the fact that it was sung while people waited to have their grain ground. An example of the *gaita gallega* would be this refrain to one of the poems in *Cantares:*

> *Fun ô mohiño*
> *d' ó meu compadre,*
> *fun pó-lo vento,*
> *vin pó-lo aire.* (289)

("I went to the mill/ of my good friend,/ I went by the wind,/ I came back by the air.")

The *triada* or *triada bárdica* (bardic triad or tambourine song) consists of a tercet of eight-syllable lines, with assonant rhyme in first and third lines:

> *Campanas de Bastabales,*
> *cando vos oyo tocar,*
> *mórrome de soidades.* (294)

("Bells of Bastabales,/ when I hear you ring,/ I die of loneliness.")

Another form of popular origin used in *Cantares* is the parallelistic song. Parallelism is an ancient device, many examples of which can be found in the medieval *cancioneiros*. The motif and its answering echo suggest that it was sung by alternate voices. A parallelistic song begins with a pair of rhymed lines plus a refrain; these lines, with slight variations, are repeated in the second stanza. The third stanza then begins with the second line of the first, adding a new element in its second line, which is then repeated with variations as in the first set, and so on. This form allows for the construction of an infinitely extensible chain of connected sentiments. Represented schematically, an example of a simple parallelistic song would go: A B C/A B C/ B D C/ B D C. The refrain, "C" in this example, is invariable throughout the composition.

Among the meters common to Spanish poetry as well is the octosyllable or *romance*, the most natural and harmonious line in the Iberian languages. It is the basis for the *copla* or quatrain of eight-syllable lines rhymed alternately in assonance, or occasionally with consonant rhyme. Long series of these units can be joined together for narrative compositions, as in the traditional Spanish ballad, also called *romance*. Present in *Cantares* also are examples of shorter lines: *seguidillas*, or four-line stanzas with lines of seven and five, eight and six, or six and four syllables in length; *romancillos* or quatrains of lines of five, six, or seven syllables; and *endechas* or four-line stanzas of six or seven syllables per line. Literary meters with more elaborate stanza forms and consonant rhyme schemes also occur: *décimas,* consisting of ten-line stanzas of octosyllables; octaves with lines of eight, eleven, or twelve syllables per line; and others. The rhyme is, for the most part, assonant. This rhyming of vowels, so fluid and effortless in the Romance tongues, is most in keeping with the popular inspiration and tone of *Cantares.* Suggestions of tension and agitation or resolution and peace can be achieved by the use of masculine (accented) or feminine (unaccented) rhyme. Consonant rhyme, when it occurs, is unforced and melodic.

The total stylistic effect of *Cantares* is not that Rosalía did research on prosody or painstakingly counted syllables and consulted rhyming dictionaries, but rather that she followed easily and without selfconsciousness the simple, traditional devices of repetition and coincidence of sounds and ideas. She captures the poetic qualities of the Galician language, with its colorful turns of phrase, capacity for contraction and prolongation, caressing diminutives, and onomatopoeic possibilities.

V   *Galicia: Nature, People, Customs*

Like the folk repertoire from which they spring, the themes of *Cantares* run the gamut of human experience. Gaiety prevails in the exuberance of nature, the spirit of youth, the zest for life, and the gentle humor. The more somber themes of sorrow and tragedy, nostalgia, and remorse find expression as well. All of the poems are infused with the tenderness of the Galician temperament, in consonance with Rosalía's own. The most dominant impression is of joy, vitality, and color. The pages give off the fresh aroma of wheat and pines, swirl with the colors of bright costumes and flowers, and resound with the lively notes of flute (*zampona*) and bagpipe (*gaita*). The animation produced by numerous verbs and adverbs and the use of short, quick meters; the living quality of the speech; and the rich suggestiveness of onomatopoeic words make the poems come alive and immerse the reader in a dynamic and sensory experience. The emotions conveyed are elemental—joy, fear, loneliness—and elicit immediate and direct response.

The book is intended as a tribute to Galicia, its beauties and its language, and as a defense against the ignorant and unjust opinions of its detractors. This intent is clearly stated in the prologue, where Rosalía soars into lyrical descriptions of Galician nature and culture, and unleashes a bitter diatribe against the ill treatment that Galicians receive in the rest of Spain. Her greatest concern, she states, was "to reproduce the true spirit of our people . . ." (". . . *puxen ó mayor coidado en reprodusir ó verdadeiro esprito d' ó noso pobo . . .*" 263).

The poems reiterate this intent. In the opening song, the bagpipe girl avows: "A more beautiful place/ never was on this earth . . ." ("*Lugar máis hermoso/ non houbo na terra . . .*" 267), and promises to sing the sweet songs of Galicia in its soft, melodious tongue. The resentment against Castile is vehemently expressed in the poems "*Castellana de Castilla*" ("Castilian Lady from Castile," XXIII, 326) and "*Castellanos de Castilla*" ("Castilians from Castile," XXVIII, 347). The latter begins with a popular couplet, and Rosalía adds: "May God grant, Castilians,/ Castilians whom I abhore,/ that rather the Galicians should die,/ than to go to you for bread." ("*Premita Dios, castellanos,/ castellanos que aborreço,/ qu' antes os gallegos morran/ qu' ir a pedirvos sustento.*" 348).

Nature is a constant element in *Cantares gallegos*, both as context and participant of the human drama. The folk tradition treats man as a part of nature. He seeks harmony with it, rejoices in its beauty and abundance, and fears its violence and destruction. There is a close connection between natural phenomena and events in human life, and nature provides metaphors and symbols to describe man's abstract concepts or psychic realities. Galician literature has always exquisitely interpreted nature, reflecting the Galician's intense awareness of and loving relationship with his environment. Frequently in traditional lyrics, the poet or speaker will converse with an object of nature, or express the wish to become or to fuse with it—to fly or flow or touch as wind or stream or grass, thus transcending distance, time, and his own physical limitations. Rosalía, though not of the folk, could enter wholeheartedly into this spirit of wonder and delight. The nature she depicts is a real and experienced nature, to which she responds deeply and passionately.

The poems of *Cantares* display a lively assortment of character types, portrayed with charm and humor. Rosalía's extensive use of dialogue and monologue allows the characters to express themselves directly and intimately, and her sure sense of language reproduces their speech with vivid realism. In poem number III, a wise and canny old woman and a pert young girl converse—a variation on the age-old theme of youth meets age. The old woman's speech is a string of aphorisms which would rival Sancho Panza's. The girl listens with wonder and curiosity and plies her for stories and songs, in return for which she offers food and shelter (271–75). In number VIII, a seductive "bonny bagpiper," local Don Juan of all the festivals, lures and deceives the girls, who flock to him like moths to a flame (289–90). A rustic recruit writes to his girl back home, boasting of his fine blue and gold uniform and proud of his education—he has lost his fear of books and can write with nice big letters (XXIV, 329–31). A chatty mother bustles about her domestic tasks and fondly scolds her children (XXIX, 357–60). A lazy wife puts off her work because every day belongs to some saint or other (XXXVI, 377–78). Two comrades merrily drink themselves to death under the spout of the keg (XXXVII, 378–81). A long folk tale in verse, of Rosalía's own invention (though faithful to the vein of folk literature), relates the story of Vidal, a poor man dependent on the reluctant charity of others. He is not invited to the customary feast when the hogs are slaughtered (a masterpiece of genre realism). Vidal eventually falls into fortune, slaughters his own hog, and carries a string of aromatic sausages past the stingy neighbors' houses without sharing with them (XXV, 332–43).

Religious observances and festivals, so much a part of the life of the folk, are represented with keen observation and sensitivity. The familiar camaraderie enjoyed by the people with their domestic saints provides the anecdote for two charming compositions. In number V, a little seamstress offers the saint's statue her earrings and necklace if the saint will teach her to *puntear*—which can mean both "to stitch" and "to keep time to music." The saint warns her about dancing and idle hands; the girl doesn't give her the necklace either (277–81). In another poem (XIII), a young girl asks San Antonio, patron of love, for a man; she'll take him "even if he is no bigger than a grain of wheat, is lame and has no arms." Her philosophy is: "Even if he is knock-kneed, it's good to have a man around." ("*Que zamb' ou trenco,/ sempr' é bó ter un home/ para un remedio.*" 300–302).

In a tumult of color and movement, Rosalía describes the festival of Our Lady of the Ship (*Nossa Señora da Barca*), celebrated in Mugía (La Coruña) on September 8. On this windlashed coast clings a small fishing village, site of the shrine of Our Lady of the Ship.

According to legend, the Miraculous Virgin arrived there in a ship of stone to comfort St. James, who was preaching to the pagans. Three huge stones of unusual formation, sculptured by wind and wave, suggest the shapes of a sail, mast, and tiller. One of the stones is flat and delicately balanced and is said to move and sing when the *muiñeira* is danced on its surface, if the dancers are in a state of grace.[5] Rosalía attended this festival in 1853, and her personal impressions lend vividness to the poem as she describes the costumes of visitors assembled from all the villages of Galicia, the sound of bells and music and the bustle of activity. She retells the legend in the poem, and the rock, on this occasion, does indeed whirl and sing.

A miracle performed by the Virgin Mary, reminiscent of those recounted in the Middle Ages by Alfonso X and Gonzalo de Berceo, is narrated in poem number XX, "Hush, my baby, hush" (*"Hora, meu menino, hora,"* 315–19). A young girl, Rosa, is tending a baby whose mother is absent. The child is hungry, the night stormy, and the mother tarries long. The Holy Virgin appears and nurses the child. Supernatural forces are not always benevolent. Dark powers exist, surrounded by fear and superstition, which must be placated or warded off with prayers and charms. A girl passing through a cemetery on a dark night is frightened by an owl, a diabolical bird which seems to sense the "sinful love" she has in her heart. She breathes a fervent "Ave María" and shouts a defiant "I'm not afraid of you, owl!" (XVI, 306–307). The old woman of poem number III, mentioned above, warns her young companion of the dangers of the sinful world. The girl, with her spine tingling, vows not to leave her village without scapularies, holy medals, and amulets to protect her from witches (274).

VI *Love and Sorrow*

Love in its many manifestations is a perennial theme of popular poetry. Many of the motifs which appealed to Rosalía deal with this theme. The joy of reciprocal love is dramatized in number IV, *"—Cantan os galos pr' ó día;/ érguete, meu ben, e vaite. . . ."* ("The cocks sing at break of day;/ arise my love, and go. . . ." 275), a tender *alborada* or dawn song. The rustic Romeo and Juliet part at dawn, with caressing endearments and promises of "happily ever after." Less fortunate lovers may be separated by emigration or other circumstances. Such is the case in number XIX, which strongly suggests the medieval *cantigas d' amigo*. A lovelorn lass, whose beloved has gone to Brazil, sheds her tears into the river so that they will flow out to sea as messages to him. She wishes that she could become a tear and go to him on the waves (314–15).

Love may also be unrequited, betrayed, or guilty. Another girl, in number IX, laments the indifference of her sweetheart. She has been told by the priest that her passion is a sin, but with an earthy innocence, she cannot accept that anything so natural and beautiful can be sinful. Candidly sensual, she wishes she were the grass and flowers he lies upon and the dew that moistens him: "Oh God! If I could be a flower/ like those he lay upon . . . !/ Or the grass which at that moment/ had him in close embrace! . . ." (*"¡Meu Dios! ¡Quén froliña fora,/ das d' aquelas . . .!/ ¡Quén as erbas qu'en tal hora,/ o tiñan pretiño d' elas! . . ."* 292). Love can be a lifelong devotion, even though the beloved is absent because of emigration or death, as in *"Qu' á rula que viudou"* ("The Widowed Turtledove," XXVI, 343–45). This is a Galician variant of the ancient theme of the faithful widow, which appears in the Spanish ballad *"Fonte frida"* ("Cold Fountain"). In Rosalía's version, the suitor is not depicted as the "treacherous nightingale" of the Spanish poem, but as an admirer who sincerely praises the widow's beauty and pleads his love. She replies that for her, love is dead and she must live alone in mourning.

In her treatment of the theme of love can be seen Rosalía's sensitive rapport with the folk, who know love as both real and ideal. Be it corresponded and fulfilled, or impossible and tragic, the touchstone is always the delights of togetherness, the joy and warmth of human affections on both a spiritual and physical plane. Love is not removed from nature, but part of its exuberance and harmony.

Another theme which moved Rosalía deeply was that of emigration—"exile" to the Galicians. Economic necessity has down through the ages forced the emigrant to wrench himself from all that he loves for prolonged and sometimes permanent residence in a strange environment where he suffers intense longing for home. Those he has left behind worry and grieve, their own lives shadowed by loneliness and sorrow. The popular quatrain which came to Rosalía's mind during one of her own "exiles" and which gave rise to the book *Cantares gallegos* is a poignant expression of the emigrant's farewell: "Farewell, rivers, farewell, springs,/ farewell little brooks,/ farewell, light of my eyes,/ I know not when we'll meet again." (*"Adiós ríos, adiós fontes,/ adiós regatos pequenos/ adiós vista dos meus ollos,/ non sei cándo nos veremos."* XV, 304–306). Throughout Rosalía's gloss, the emigrant enunciates his emotion by the simple and loving enumeration of the objects of his intimate world—fields, garden, trees, river, village—and culminates with the heartbreaking farewell to home and beloved.

Love and sorrow mingle in the emotion of *saudade,* one of the most Galician and Lusitanian of sentiments. It is closely associated with the theme of emigration. The laments of both those who leave and those who stay are filled with this particular sorrow. The word *saudade,* which appears in *Cantares* in a variety of dialectal spellings, such as *soidades* and *soidás,* derives from Latin *solitatem,* and is cognate to Spanish *soledad* and English "solitude." In Galician and Portuguese it has acquired such complexities and subtleties that it is virtually untranslatable. Simply stated, it connotes a longing for someone or something absent. The recollection of this beloved person, place, or whatever it may be, produces a bitter-sweet sentiment, at once sad and comforting. Sometimes the feeling has no specific cause, but is a vague and indefinable sense of solitude and loss. Among the Galicians it can reach such intensity that it is termed *morriña* or "little death." Numerous definitions can be found and treatises have been written on the subject.[6] It is most directly and effectively communicated, however, through the plaintive songs and lyrics so characteristic of the Galician-Portuguese tradition.

Saudade is a sorrow produced by love, and is quickened by an affective stimulus which evokes the memory of that which is absent. This stimulus is often music or bells, whose sound transcends time and space and unites in the subjective reality the sad present with the happiness remembered: "Bells of Bastabales,/ when I hear you ring,/ I die of *soidades."* (*"Campanas de Bastabales,/ cando vos oyo tocar,/ mórrome de soidades."* XI, 294). One of the most lyrical and moving expressions of the longing of one who is away from home and suffering from intense *saudades* or *morriña* is the poem "Airs of my land" (*"Airiños, airiños, aires,"* XVII, 308–11), in which the word *airiños* conveys the dual meanings of "breezes" and "songs." In this poem the personal emotion of Rosalía can be strongly felt:

. . . .

Sweet Galician airs,
which take away all care,
enchantors of the waters,
lovers of the groves,
music of the green stalks
of the corn in our fields,
happy little companions,
bustle of all the fairs,
take me on your wings,
like a light, dry leaf.
Do not let me die here,
oh airs of my land,
for I think that when I'm dead
I shall sigh for it. . . .

. . . .

Doçe galleguiños aires,
quitadoiriños de penas,
encantadores d' as auguas,
amantes d' as arboredas,
música d' as verdes canas
do millo d' as nosas veigas,
alegres compañeiriños,
run-run de tódalas festas
levaime nas vosas alas
com' unha folliña seca.
Non permitás qu' aquí morra,
airiños da miña terra,
qu' ainda penso, que de morta
ei de sospirar por ela. . . . (310)

Throughout *Cantares gallegos*, the poet remains, for the most
part, unobtrusive, speaking through her personae and objectivizing
through dramatization, immersing herself in the spirit of the collective lyrics. Occasionally, however, the guise is dropped and she is
openly personal. In the gloss to "How the gentle rain falls" (*"Cómo
chove mihudiño,"* XXXII, 364–70), the melancholy mood suggested
by the reference to the rain evokes her own fond sentiments for
familiar landmarks. She calls up memories of her mother and of the
Castro ancestral home, "Arretén," and dwells on the theme of "they

have gone" and "they are no more." Her omniscient point of view can be detected in her suggestion that the superstitions so real to the folk are the projections of psychological states. The old woman of number III remarks to the young girl: ". . . we are for ourselves/ the most dangerous evil spirits." (". . . *somos nos para nos/ as lurpias máis enemigas.*" 274); and the girl frightened in the cemetery (XVI) identifies the owl with her own guilty conscience. Rosalía's presence is sensed throughout in the choice of themes which most moved her and in the convincing quality of their utterance.

In *Cantares gallegos,* the brief lyrics of the folk, with their universal appeal, power of suggestion, and graceful charm, were gathered and interpreted by the sensitivity and imagination of a creative mind. What Rosalía has done most beautifully in *Cantares* is to capture the luminous treasure of a refined popular poetry and filter it through her own exquisite sensibility. Her temperament and fervor infuse these unforgettable lyrics with shimmering intensity.

CHAPTER 6

Follas novas (New Leaves)

FROM 1863 to 1880, Rosalía produced several works in prose. A short story in Galician, *"Conto gallego"* ("Galician Tale"), was written in 1863, but was not published until 1923.[1] This is her only prose piece in dialect (except for the prefaces to the two books of poetry in Galician) and may have been intended as part of a collection of tales which she never compiled. In 1866, two prose pieces, *Ruinas (Ruins)*, a novelette, and *El cadiceño (The Man from Cádiz)*, a satirical sketch, appeared, and an article, *"Las literatas"* ("Literary Women"), was published in *Almanaque de Galicia*, Lugo. Her most ambitious novel, *El caballero de las botas azules (The Gentleman of the Blue Boots)*, came out in 1867. She continuously wrote poems during these years, some of which were later to comprise the collections *Follas novas (New Leaves)* and *En las orillas del Sar (On the Banks of the River Sar)*. These were busy years as wife and mother as well; all of her children, except for the eldest, Alejandra (1859), were born between 1869 and 1877.

I *Genesis, Intent and Sources*

Follas novas (New Leaves), Rosalía's second volume of verse in Galician, appeared in 1880. It represents an accumulation of poetry written over a ten year span, begun in Simancas during one of the residences there with her husband and continued in La Coruña and Santiago. In her foreword to the book, Rosalía states that the poems had not been intended for publication, and had been hastily and reluctantly assembled for the press because of "old commitments." These commitments were her feeling of obligation to follow the reception of *Cantares* and to satisfy her debt to the Galician people with one more book in dialect. There also seems to have been pressure from Murguía and the other Galician enthusiasts to try for another success.

The book is dedicated to the Society for the Welfare of Galician Natives in Havana (*Sociedad de Beneficiencia d' os Naturales de Galicia n' Habana*), one of many such organizations created in the American Republics by emigrants from the various cultural regions of Spain. Rosalía had many admirers among the members of the Galician societies in America, particularly those of Havana and Buenos Aires. The prologue was written by the eminent historian, critic, and statesman, Emilio Castelar (1832–1899).

Rosalía's own foreword is simply entitled "A Few Words by the Author" (*"Duas palabras d' a autora"*), and is one of her most revealing personal and literary documents. Here she characterizes the poems as "poor offspring of my sorrow" (*"probes enxendros d' a miña tristura"* 410). Upon re-examining them after more than ten years of agitated life and constant ill health, she sees that they are "incomplete and poor" and fears that the public will find them tiresome and monotonous. However, her verses can only reflect her sorrows: "Written in the desert of Castile, thought and felt in the solitary wastes of Nature and of my heart, children of the captivity of hours of sickness and absences . . ." (*"Escritos n' ò deserto de Castilla, pensados e sentidos n' as soidades d' á Natureza e d' ò meu corazón, fillos cativos d' as horas de enfermedade e d' ausencias . . ."* 410).

"Sadness," she continues, "is the muse of our times," and one she knows well. Nonetheless, she does not presume to write a "transcendental" book. Leave that to the men, the philosophers and scholars; as a woman it behooves her to speak of the emotions—her own and those of others, shared and intermingled—for that is her realm. When women undertake serious studies, they deceive only the frivolous with the artifice of clever form. The true scholars will perceive the lack of substance, and that she would avoid at all costs: "In the realms of speculation, as in those of art, there is nothing more useless nor cruel than the mediocre." (*"E n' os dominios d' á especulación, como n' os d' o arte, nada máis inutil nin cruel d' o que ó vulgar."* 411). This is not an admission of feminine inferiority, for she does not draw ranks of relative worth between speculation and feeling, but rather a declaration of her artistic independence, a refusal to tread the footsteps of men or the women who imitate them, a horror of being labeled *"literata"* (literary woman), *"poetisa"* (poetess) or *"marisabida"* (bluestocking), pejorative terms applied to women who dared to be intellectual or artistic. Intellec-

tual pursuits are not natural nor important to the particular woman
who is herself; her aspiration is only to express her soul in "simple
poetry, which finds, at times, in a felicitous expression, in a fortunate idea, that nameless thing which flies straight as an arrow,
penetrates our flesh, makes us quiver, and resounds in the sorrowful
heart like another ay! in response to the long moan which the sorrows of the earth continually arouse within us." (". . . *simple poesía,
qu' encontr' as veces n' un-ha expresión feliz, n' un-ha idea afer-
tunada, aquela cousa sin nome que vai direita come frecha, traspasa
as nosas carnes, fainos estremecer, e resona n' a alma dorida como
un outro ¡ay! que responde ô largo xemido que decote levantan en
nos os dôres d' a terra.*" 411). This statement, as well as the poetry it
defines, relates her spiritually to the line of inner poets, particularly
to Bécquer, her contemporary, and to the later writers of the Generation of 1898.

Rosalía prepares the reader for the change of mood in *Follas* (*New
Leaves*), which is not the product of the same inspiration as *Cantares*. Whereas the former had the springlike quality of hope, youth,
and innocence, the latter was written in physical and spiritual exile,
and the light which illumines it is crepuscular and autumnal. Galicia
is no longer the object and animating force, but rather the cir-
cumstance and the backdrop. *New Leaves* does not treat the quaint,
picturesque, and festive aspects, but focuses on the suffering of
Galicia, particularly of the Galician women, fused with the poet's
own suffering. The sources are, to a certain extent, Galician life and
lore, but the poems for the most part derive from her own intimate
experiences. *New Leaves* contains some of Rosalía's most significant
poetry and represents an important contribution to the literature of
the peninsula. It has escaped more widespread attention not only
because of the language, but because of the content as well. Like
any really significant artistic landmark, it was not recognized until
its time had come. It is not primarily a regional work, but a truly
universal poetic achievement and harbinger of a new introspective
age.

The title has double implications, as *follas* can mean "leaves" or
"pages," but the nature imagery is uppermost. The poet smiles
ironically: "There they go, then, the *New Leaves*, which might better be called old, because they are, and last, because the debt in
which I seemed to be with my land having been paid, it is not likely
that I shall write more verses in the mother tongue." ("*Alá van,
pois, as* FOLLAS NOVAS, *que mellor se dirían vellas, porque ò son, e*

últimas, porque pagada va á deuda en que me parecía estar c' o á miña terra, difícil é que volva a escribir máis versos n' á lengua materna." 413).

II *Language*

The Galician language is used in *Follas* but no longer for the sake of the folk who will not read the verses written "because of them but not to them." (413). It will be the last book in Galician, and the poet will henceforth consider the debt she felt herself in to be paid. The muted statement quoted above of Rosalía's intent to write no more verses in the mother tongue is given more vehement expression in a letter to Murguía in 1881. An editor had evidently approached her for another book in Galician and Murguía was in favor of it. Rosalía informs Murguía that he is to communicate to the editor "my resolution not to take up the pen again for anything pertaining to this land, nor much less write in Galician . . ." (". . . *mi resolución de no volver a coger la pluma para nada que pertenezca a este país, ni menos escribir en gallego . . .*" 1552). The reasons for this hostility can only be conjectured, but perhaps relate to resentment at some sort of personally leveled criticism, weariness at fame, or refusal to be further used as prime exhibit or to serve as publicity for the Galician cause.

In *Cantares* Galician was the naturally suited vehicle to reproduce the popular motifs and provide continuity between them and the poet's glosses. The verbal portrait of the people was painted in the colors of their own speech. In *New Leaves* the language must accomplish quite a different task; it must convey the subjective and meditative content of the poet's deepest spiritual and intellectual experiences. *Cantares* retained the oral quality of song and speech; *Follas* is meant to be read and reflected upon. In Rosalía's hands, Galician proves to be an effective literary instrument—musical, suggestive, intimate, and powerful. If it once expressed the highest lyrical sentiments of the peninsula, it does so again in Rosalía's poems and becomes a truly modern tongue.

III *Organization and Forms*

Follas is a long collection—139 poems of varying lengths—representing themes as deep and tangled as the poet's thoughts and emotions. The organization of the book reflects the author's admission that the collection was of loose poems composed over a ten year span and not originally intended for publication. There are five divisions entitled: *"Vaguedás"* ("Reveries"); *"¡Do íntimo!"* ("From the Heart"); *"Da terra"* ("From the Land"); *"Varia"* ("Miscellany"); *"As viudas d'os vivos e as viudas d'os mortos"* ("Widows of the Living and of the Dead"). These titles give some indication of thematic grouping, but the division is not strict.

The collection includes many compositions of traditional nature and continues some of the forms found in *Cantares*. In this book, however, Rosalía is not restricted to popular models, and utilizes all the forms of the Hispanic tradition—particularly the effortless, fluid, serene lines of the *romance* (eight syllables) and the *silva* (eleven and seven syllables). There is no strict adherence to set forms, however, for she often gives these basic meters her individual touch. A tendency begins to appear toward the use of the longer meters, such as *arte mayor* (twelve syllables), which is sometimes combined with its hemistych in a *pie quebrado* ("broken foot") form, and *alejandrinos* (Alexandrine or fourteen-syllable lines). What is unusual in *Follas* is the use of varying line lengths for metrical combinations generally considered unsuitable and unharmonious, such as eight with ten or eleven syllables or eight with fourteen. The effect is striking, and follows shifts of emotion and fluctuations of thought, reflecting reality which is not stable or predictable. The syntax does not adhere to the simple patterns of oral clarity and folksong cadence, but is rearranged in a more literary manner.

The innovations in versification with which Rosalía has been credited are not calculated experiments in an effort to be original or daring (as were those of Darío and the Modernists); hers are the result of emotions seeking rhythmic expression. Content begets form; form enhances and is an integral part of content. In this, Rosalía coincides with the Symbolists' and Modernists' search for freedom of expression, the desire to reproduce an "ideal melody" unhampered by prosody. There is also a noticeable affinity with the Symbolists in fluidity and musical suggestivity of her verse. She characterizes the music of the poems of *Follas* in its relationship to the content in one of the initial poems of the collection:

> You will say of these lines, and it is so,
> that they have a strange, unusual harmony,
> that in them the ideas shine faintly
>   like elusive melodies
>   which burst forth for an instant

and quickly disappear,
that they resemble the uncertain mist
which rolls in the depths of the meadows,
and the monotonous whisper of the pines
  on the stormy sea shore.

I can only tell you that my songs
thus issue in confusion from my soul,
as issues from the thick oak groves
    at break of day,
      such sound one cannot tell
      if it is stirring of the breeze
      or kisses of the flowers
or wild mysterious harmonies
      which lost in this sad world
are searching for the sky.

(*Diredes d' estos versos, y é verdade,*
que tên extraña insólita armonía,
que n' eles as ideas brilan pálidas
      cal errantes muxicas
      qu' estalan por istantes
      que desparecen xiña,
que s' asomellan á parruma incerta
que voltexa n' ò fondo d' as curtiñas,
y ò susurro monótono d' os pinos
      d' a veira-mar bravía.

Eu direivos tan sô qu' os meus cantares
así sân en confuso d' alma miña,
como sai d' as profundas carballeiras,
      ô comenzar d' o día,
      romor que non se sabe
      s' é rebuldar d' as brisas,
      si son beixos d' as frores,
s' agrestes misteriosas armonías
      que n' este mundo triste
o camiño d' o ceu buscan perdidas.) (IV, 416)

IV Galicia, the "Dolorous Epic"

In her foreword, "A Few Words by the Author," Rosalía has
expounded the theme of *dolor*, which is to dominate the book.
There are repeated references to suffering, sadness, misfortune, and
grief—all of which are implied by the word *dolor*. On its various

levels, *dolor* is the central and unifying element of *Follas novas*, and embraces psychological suffering as well as physical, the ills of man's mortal state and the anguishes of his mind and soul.

Rosalía exclaims in the foreword: "There is so much suffering in this dear Galician land!" (*"¡E sófrese tanto n' esta querida terra gallega!"* 412). After ennumerating the specific ills which beset her land, she concludes: "It would take greater than I to sing for you with all its truth and poetry such a simple yet dolorous epic." ("*. . . quéreas mayores de quen haya de cantarnos con toda á sua verdade e poesía tan sencilla como dolorosa epopeya.*" 413). In her treatment of Galicia and its people, the poet now focuses on their suffering. Although she establishes esthetic distance through dramatization and the creation of *personae*, the poems are objective and subjective at the same time, for what she observes and selects is conditioned by her own predilections and empathy, as she confesses: ". . . I can no longer distinguish what there is in my book of my own sorrows, or of those of others, although I well might claim them all as mine . . ." (*". . . iñoro ó que haxa n' ò meu libro d' os propios pesares, ou d' os alleos, anque ben podo telos todos por meus . . ."* 411).

New Leaves contains sketches of popular inspiration which depict characters and customs reminiscent of those of *Cantares*, yet there is a note of poverty and suffering which underlies the charm and quaintness. Amid the liveliness and gentle humor of the portraits, there is hunger, deprivation, and the fear of nature and destiny, to be warded off with superstitious charms. In the poem entitled "Home Sweet Home" (*"Miña casiña, meu lar"* 495), inspired by a popular refrain, a woman returns to her humble cottage after walking from Santiago to Padrón through a stormy night. The cupboard is bare, the hearth cold. She builds a fire with straw from her bed, finds meager ingredients for soup, and sings contentedly of her home sweet home. The persistent pluck of the Galician peasant and his joy in victory over circumstances shine through.

The nearness of the supernatural and the awe that it inspires, and the mingling of religion and superstition, are illustrated in "Foolish Pride" (*"Soberba"*), whose title refers to the presumptuousness of the human being who thinks he can defy the powers of God and nature. As a storm approaches, a frightened family tries to placate God's wrath with candles, olive leaves, and prayers, and search their own hearts for possible offenses which might have incurred the misfortune (497–98).

A long *costumbrista* (local color) narrative, "The Poor Old Deaf
Woman" ("*¡A probiña qu' esta xorda . . .!*" 498), describes a clever
old woman (sister to the loquacious character of *Cantares*, III, 271–
75) who seeks food and lodging in a wealthy house where a party is
going on. She feigns deafness, and, unable to hear the hostess protest that the house is already crowded, gains admission to the circle
of poor people around the fire. Her secret is quickly discovered, but
her wit charms the hosts and other guests and she enjoys one night
of warmth and plenty.

The tragedy of unwilling departure for dangerous and unknown
destiny, a perennial theme of the Galician, is movingly portrayed.
For the men who depart, it means leaving the familiar and beloved
country, sweethearts, and families, to face "the abyss" or the
"cemetery of Havana." For the women left behind, their lot is hardship and loneliness:

> This one goes and that one goes,
> and all of them, all of them go;
> Galicia, you are left with no men
> who can work your soil.
> You have, instead, orphaned children
> and solitary fields,
> and mothers who have no sons,
> and sons whose fathers are gone.
> And you have hearts that suffer
> long mortal absences,
> widows of the living and the dead
> whom no one can console.

> *(Este vaise y aquel vaise,*
> *e todos, todos se van;*
> *Galicia, sin homes quedas*
> *que te poidan traballar.*
> *Tês, en cambio, orfos e orfas*
> *e campos de soledad,*
> *e nais que non teñen fillos*
> *e fillos que no tén pais.*
> *E tês corazóns que sufren*
> *longas ausencias mortás,*
> *viudas de vivos e mortos*
> *que ninguén consolará.)* (V, 523)

A more tragic view of love appears in *New Leaves*, with love often the source of sorrow through separation, disillusionment, abandonment, and all the bitter mysteries of relations between men and women. Frequently the love theme is dramatized in a brief dialogue between lovers, without exposition or conclusion, caught at the most intense moment of emotion. The setting is not dawn after a happy night of love, but nocturnal and bleak; the love is not free and hopeful, but furtive and anxious. Rosalía usually presents the side of the woman, be she one who sacrifices security and honor for love (465–66; 466–67), one whose passion is not requited (478), or one who waits and hopes for her beloved's return (530). The men may leave heartbroken and remain faithful, but more often they take a cynical view, "Antona is there, but I have Rosa here" (542). Some poems have neither situation nor narrative, but hauntingly express the bitter and enduring sorrow of impossible love:

> Take me to that crystalline fountain
>   where we drank together
> the pure waters which quenched
> thirst of love and flame of desire.
> Take me by the hand as in other days . . .
>   But no, for I am afraid
>   to see in the crystal liquid
>   the shadow of that black
> disillusionment, without cure or consolation
>   which time has put between us.
>
> *(Lévame a aquela fonte cristaiña*
>   *onde xuntos bebemos*
> *as purísimas auguas qu' apagaban*
> *sede d' amor e llama de deseyos.*
> *Lévame pol-a man cal n' otros días . . .*
>   *Mais non, que teño medo*
>   *de ver n' ò cristal líquido*
>   *a sombra d' aquel negro*
> *desengano sin cura nin consolo*
>   *qu' antr' os dous puxo ò tempo.)* (437)

The nature and landscape of Galicia are a constant presence in *New Leaves*, but have taken on a different function. Scenic description is not merely for its own sake, but has become the principal source of imagery for Rosalía's poetic expression. Galicia is, as she states in her foreward, "always in the background: for if the spirit cannot remove its wrapping of flesh, except in death, neither can the poet separate himself from the ambience in which he lives and the Nature which surrounds him . . ." (". . . *sempre ò fondo d' ò cuadro: que si non pode se non c' a morte despirse ò esprito d' as envolturas d' á carne menos pode o poeta prescindir d' ò medio en que vive e d' á Natureza que ó rodea . . .*" 411). Nature provides elements from visible external reality to represent and communicate the invisible inner world. Familiar natural features are removed from unique and specific context and are abstracted to represent spiritual values. Thus river, tree, sea, or fog call forth a visual image and emotional response, but also signify concepts such as time, life, destiny, or mystery. The landscape, recognizable in its components, has become, to employ Fernando Pessoa's term, a "landscape of the soul."[2]

V *Spiritual Suffering*

The reader becomes aware that *New Leaves* is the testimony of a troubled soul and that he is witnessing the unfolding of a deep psychological drama. In the evolution of Rosalía's poetic work, this second volume represents a phase of disintegration, struggle, and despair. In the language of the mystics, it would parallel the "dark night of the soul," the anguished experience of terror and nothingness which the mystic suffers in his quest for enlightenment and ecstasy. In psychological terms, it corresponds to the suffering of the disturbed psyche, the painful exploration of the unconscious in search of the self and spiritual wholeness. Jolande Jacobi, incorporating words of C. G. Jung, describes the process of probing for inner knowledge in search of "salvation" or "healing" of the psyche: "Only a few are willing and able to travel a path of salvation. 'And these few tread the path only from inner necessity, not to say suffering, for it is sharp as the edge of a razor.' "[3] Rosalía undertook such a path (she frequently employs the images of road and journey in her poems) alone and probably not consciously aware that she was doing so. This does not propose to be a psychological treatise, but the insights offered by studies of psychology applied to Rosalía's works cannot be overlooked in the attempt to unravel the complexities of her intimate poetry. It is no coincidence that *New Leaves* has received more attention and greater comprehension in a psychologically aware age.

In many poems of this collection, the world of established values
is confused and chaotic; reality is shifting and unstable. Besides
influencing verbal content, this is reflected stylistically in the irregular rhythms of the lines, the frequency of questions and negations,
and the use of ellipses which trail off into silence. There is a paradox-
ical reversal of values: hope is a "mortal enemy" (418); the light and
beauty of nature contrast with the darkness of the poet's soul (438);
happiness is fearful (436). The poet is bewildered and haunted by
fear of vague, impending misfortune *(desgracia)*:

> What happens all around me?
> What happens to me that I do not know?
> I am afraid of some thing
> which lives but cannot be seen.
> I am afraid of treacherous misfortune
> which comes, but one knows not from whence it comes.

> *(¿Qué pasa ò redor de min?*
> *¿Qué me pasa qu' eu non sei?*
> *Teño medo d' un-ha cousa*
> *que vive e que non se ve.*
> *Teño medo à desgracia traidora*
> *que ven, e que nunca se sabe ónde ven.)* (VI, 417)

Dark principles prevail in *Follas*, indicative of the lost and tortured state of her spirit. Colors are muted, often reduced to a play of
light and dark. The poet leaves the "insolent light" of the external
world and seeks the solitary shadows of her soul:

> (. . . .

> Thenceforth I sought the shadows
>   most black and deep,
> and I sought them in vain, for always
> after the night I encountered the dawn . . .
> Only searching in the darkness of myself
>   and entering shadowy realms,
> did I see never-ending night
>   in my own lonely soul.

>   . . . .
> *Desde entonces busquei as tiniebras*
>   *máis negras e fondas,*

e busqueinas en vano, que sempre
tras d' a noite topaba c' a aurora . . .
So en min mesma buscando n' oscuro
y entrando n' a sombra,
vin á noite que nunca s' acaba
n' á miña alma soya.) (429)

Rosalía is aware that the trouble or pain is within herself, and locates it in those traditional centers of the psyche: heart, soul, and spirit. This pain often finds its analogy in physical sensations: "How the soul aches!" ("*¡Cómo lle doy á yalma*" 540); "the sick and wounded heart" ("*o lastimado corazón enfermo*" 423); "mortal poison" ("*pezoña mortal*" 432); "A thirst. . . , a thirst/ for I know not what, which kills me" ("*Tan sô un-ha sede . . ., un-ha sede,/ d' un non sei qué, que me mata*" 420); "incurable sickness" ("*mal que non ten cura*" 491):

I have a sickness which has no cure,
a sickness born within me,
and this ferocious ailment
will carry me to my grave.

. . . .

My sickness and my suffering,
they are my heart itself,
take it from me without mercy!
And then, cause me to live!

(Teño un mal que non ten cura,
un mal que nacéu comigo,
y ese mal tan enemigo
levarám' à sepultura.

. . . .

O meu mal y ò meu sofrir,
é ò meu propio corazón,
¡quitaimo sin compasión!
Despois, ¡faceme vivir!) (491)

In the beautifully realized poem of the "thorn" ("*cravo*"), the pain is both physical and spiritual, at once detested and beloved:

Once I had a thorn
   lodged within my heart,
and I no longer recall if that thorn
   was of gold, of iron or of love.
I only know that it caused me such pain,
   that it tormented me so,
that I wept endlessly day and night
like Magdalene at Christ's Passion.
   "Dear Lord, who art all-powerful
   —I begged once of God—
give me strength to tear out
   such a painful thorn."

And He granted my prayer, and I tore it out,
   but . . . who can explain? . . . Then
   I felt no more torments
   nor knew what sorrow was;
I only knew that something was lacking
   where the thorn had come out,
and I felt something like a longing
   for that old pain . . . Dear God!
This mortal clay which enwraps the spirit,
   who can understand it, Lord!

(Una-ha vez tiven un cravo
   cravado no corazón,
y eu non m' acordo xa s' era aquel cravo
   d' ouro, de ferro ou d' amor.
Soyo sei que me fixo un mal tan fondo,
   que tanto m' atormentóu,
qu' eu día e noite sin cesar choraba
cal chorou Madalena n' a Pasión.
   "Señor, que todo ó podedes
   —pedinlle un-ha vez a Dios—,
daime valor pr' arrincar d' un golpe
   cravo de tal condiçón."

E doumo Dios e arrinqueimo,
   mais . . . ¿quén pensara? . . . Despois
   xa non sentin máis tormentos
   nin soupen qu' era delor;
soupen sô que non sei qué me faltaba
   en donde ò cravo faltóu.
e seica . . . , seica tiven soidades

> *d' aquela pena . . . ¡Bon Dios!*
> *Este barro mortal qu' envolve ò esprito,*
> *¡quén-o entenderá, Señor! . . .) (418–19)*

In the dark and lonely regions of her soul, the poet is haunted by spectral configurations. These may be terrifying phantoms, and she struggles desperately with them, or tries to flee: "Sea, with your fathomless waters,/ sky, with your inmensity,/ help me to bury/the phantom which terrifies me!" ("*¡Mar! c' as tuas auguas sin fondo,/ ¡ceo!, c' a túa inmensidá,/ o fantasma que m' aterra,/ axudádeme a enterrar.*" 435). And yet, she knows that she cannot escape, for the phantom is part of herself: ". . . but no, I carry you within me,/ frightful phantom of my own remorse!" ("*. . . mais non, dentro te levo,/ ¡fantasma pavoroso d' os meus remordementos!*" 456). She accepts this dark side of herself, her "shadow" (*"sombra"*), in an ambivalent love-hate relationship: like the thorn, it is a beloved torment. Both the shadow and the thorn, ancient and familiar symbols, universal as the ideas they contain, become very personally Rosalía's:

> When I think that you have fled,
> black shadow who haunt me,
> there at the foot of my bed
> you return to mock me.
>
> When I imagine you are gone
> you appear in the very sun,
> you are the star which shines,
> and you are the wind which moans.
>
> If they sing, it is you who sing,
> If they weep, it is you who weep;
> you are the murmur of the river
> you are the night, you are the dawn.
>
> You are all things, and in all things,
> for me and in me you dwell,
> nor will you ever leave me,
> shadow who haunt me always.
>
> *(Cando penso que te fuches,*
> *negra sombra que m' asombras,*
> *ô pe d' os meus cabezales*
> *tornas facéndome mofa.*

> *Cando maxino qu' ês ida*
> *n' ò mesmo sol te m' amostras,*
> *y eres á estrela que brila,*
> *y eres ò vento que zoa.*
>
> *Si cantan, ês ti que cantas;*
> *si choran, ês ti que choras:*
> *y ês ó marmurio d' o río*
> *y-ês á noite y ês á aurora.*
>
> *En todo estás e ti ês todo,*
> *pra min y en min mesma moras,*
> *nin m' abandonarás nunca,*
> *sombra que sempre m' asombras.)* (436)

The translation fails to capture the music of these stanzas—the effortless harmony of the eight-syllable meter with assonant rhyme in *o* in alternate lines and the crescendo-decrescendo effect of the repetition of simple phonetic elements. Nor can English duplicate the cadence of the key words *sombra* (shadow, shade, darkness) and *asombra* (from *asombrar*, to shadow, frighten, haunt) and the subtle interplay of meanings, all of which enhance the central thematic content.

VI   Road and Journey Symbolism

Another representation of the flight from torment and search for fulfillment is the road and its associated ideas of flight, journey, and quest, also universal symbols for the passage of life and psychological experience which have been assimilated and interpreted in a personal manner by the poet. The poem "From here I see a road" (*"Dend' aquí vexo un camiño"*) illustrates Rosalía's tendency to project symbolic meaning into aspects of natural reality; a white, dusty road winding through the Galician countryside past familiar landmarks comes to signify her desire to flee from herself and her sufferings. The poet contemplates the road as it winds out of sight, and imagines the scenes it will pass on its way. Then her fantasy of escape is shattered by the realization of its impossibility:

> . . . .
>
> Would I could lose myself in you
> never to find myself again . . .
> But you continue on and on,

ever toward where you must go,
and I am shackled here where
my sorrow has its roots.
I do not flee, for even though
I fled from place to place
from myself, no one, no one,
no one can set me free.

(. . . .

Que ojallá en ti me perdera
pra nunca máis m' atopar . . .
Mais ti vas indo, vas indo,
sempre para donde vas,
y eu quedo encravada en onde
arraigo ten ò meu mal.
Nin fuxo, non, que anque fuxa
d' un lugar a outro lugar
de min mesma, naide, naide,
naide me libertará.) (538)

The theme of flight is sometimes dramatized in the form of a monologue of a guilt-ridden woman fleeing from the censure of society and her own conscience. She leaves behind, and then returns to, her children, who may represent responsibilities, security, innocence, and hope. In "They howled at me as I walked along" ("*Ladraban contra min, que camiñaba,*" 432–33), the woman rushes breathlessly down the road, past the mocking eyes of passers-by, haunted by the "mortal poison" within herself. To evade the prying eyes of the people she encounters, she seeks protection of walls and deserted roads until she reaches home. Anxiously she climbs to the room where her children are sleeping peacefully under the Virgin's protection. Innocence exists, she has not contaminated it, yet she is outside and alien.

Another poem, the long narrative "The Enchantment of the Flat Stone" ("*O encanto da Pedra Chan,*" 508–13), is laden with symbolic elements capable of interpretation on many levels. It provides one of the most intriguing assemblages of clues to Rosalía's psychological drama. Without attempting here a detailed explication of the poem, a few of its suggestive possibilities will be mentioned. Folk motifs from Galician lore with archetypal content are mingled with recognizable elements from Rosalía's personal symbols. The reader enters a world of fantasy, myth, and dream.

To summarize the poem, a woman leaves her innocent children and sets out in search of "fortune" or the "coveted treasure." Nature and human life are serene and lyrical along her way. She arrives at her destination—the "flat stone where the crow perches at dawn"—and there sits a handsome gentleman dressed "in Moorish fashion." The place and nature all around are enchanted; the sky is rose colored and soft breezes blow. The charming gentleman beckons to her, smites the stone with his diamond scepter and the stone opens to reveal galleries full of gold and jewels. Before she may claim her treasure, the gentleman suggests a toast to the farewell to sorrows and the beginning of never-ending bliss. Both lower their lips to the cup, then ecstasy and torment mingle, for from the cup spring hissing serpents which fall upon the woman, biting and poisoning her. The enchantment disappears and she awakens beneath a threatening, stormy sky. The poem concludes:

> . . . .
>   And I know not what low voice murmured,
>   with the howling wind:
>   "Like you, evil treasure,
>   which the Moor left here
>   and which covetousness prizes,
>   are all earthly enchantments,
>   such great pleasures beget great evils."
>
> (. . . .
>   *E non sei que voz rouca marmuraba,*
>   *c' ò vento que soaba;*
>   *"Coma ti, mal tesouro,*
>   *que aquí deixou ò mouro*
>   *e que á cubiza alaba,*
>   *son os encantos todos terreales,*
>   *a tan grandes pracers, tan grandes males.")* (513)

Many of the motifs of the poem are recognizable elements from Galician lore (also common to other parts of the peninsula and Europe). The Moorish gentleman is a variation of the Moorish princess who guards treasures. The flat stone would correspond to the many such formations to be found in Galicia which are the site of shrines or surrounded with superstitious beliefs. Common elements of lore are treasures hidden in caves, serpents which guard treasures, and the crow, a bird of portent. The crow appears elsewhere in Rosalía's poems and perhaps represents the ominous aspects of the shadow symbol. The tendency of Rosalía to give psychological interpretations to folk motifs, which appeared in *Cantares*—for example the owl in the cemetery, XVI, 306–308—becomes more marked in *New Leaves*. In "There is no worse witch than a great sorrow" ("*N' hay peor meiga que un-ha gran pena*," 449–53), the "witchcraft" which kills the girl Marianiña is really a guilty and unhappy love; the "Mother of all the witches" who lives in the deep forest in the poem "Giant elms, myrtles . . . ," ("*Xigantescos olmos, mirtos . . .*," 456–57) represents a scapegoat of collective guilt.

"The Enchantment of the Flat Stone" might also be given a moralistic interpretation—disillusionment with mortal pleasures, punishment for sensuality and covetousness, and the presumptuous human quest for life and knowledge. The motifs could likewise be interpreted as sexual images, connected with the love-guilt preoccupations of *La flor*. The colors and soft breezes of the setting are very sensuous; there is the expectation of pleasure; the seductive gentleman with his sceptre is a Mephistopheles figure which could represent sensual forces; the pair drinks from the cup of ecstasy, from which issue the serpents of passion; the final reaction is castigation and disillusionment.

On another level, it can be seen to refer to the soul's search for wholeness and fulfillment. The treasure would then represent the elusive treasure of life, the mystic center hidden deep in the cave of the unconscious, the center of the self. The stone is the symbol of being and harmony with self; when broken or shattered, it can mean psychic disintegration. The stone of the poem bursts open "like a ripe pomegranate" (510). The serpents represent dragons of the former self, evil forces to be overcome, the snake of passions or the realm of the unconscious. The Mephistopheles figure can also be the shadow or dark self.[4] The poem ends on a note of disillusionment and frustration, indicative of the fact that Rosalía had not achieved psychic wholeness at the time she wrote *New Leaves*.

VII *Solitude and Time*

In *Cantares* time and solitude were blended in the sentiment *saudade*, the loneliness of one who remembers and longs for someone or something loved. The two components of *saudade* become more distinct as solitude and time in her second collection. The inner journey of the psyche which Rosalía has undertaken in *New Leaves* is of necessity solitary, accompanied only by other aspects of herself—spirit, shadow, soul, or phantom. She is isolated from her fellow men, who stare and mock; she refers to herself as "exile," "stranger," and "orphan" to describe this alienation. The words "alone" and "solitude" echo plaintively throughout the poems. As with the "thorn" and the "shadow," she accepts this destiny: "How sweet, yet also how sad/ is solitude!" (*"¡Qué dòce, mais qué triste,/ tamén é a soedad!"* 421).

Time perceived inwardly is a confusion of present awareness (tedium, futility), memory, and anguished sense of mortality. Linear or chronological time, the measure of man's earthly existence, ticks relentlessly by, a fleeting point between two infinite abysses, the past and eternity. She confronts the eternal human question so beautifully expressed by the French philosopher Pascal (1623–1662): "What is a man in infinity?" (*"Qu'est-ce qu'un homme dans l'infini?"*).[5] She describes this awareness in the poem "Tick-tock!, tick-tock!, in the silence of night . . ." (*"¡Tas-tis!, ¡tas-tis!, n' a silenciosa noite . . ."* 439–40):

> . . . .
> And the clock dully beating,
> like the beat of a sorrow-laden heart,
>   resounds awesomely
>   in impenetrable darkness.
> In vain the fearful eyes wander
>   ceaselessly in the dark.
> The silent instants, one by one
> go past, and silently follow
> others in their wake, falling into eternity
> as grain falls upon the grinding stone,
> and mortal eyes cannot tear away
>   the mists which veil the future.
>
> How sad is the night, and the clock, how sad,
> when the restless body and mind keep vigil!
>
> (. . . .
> *Y-a péndola no-máis xorda batendo*
> *cal bate un corazón qu' hinchan as penas,*
>   *resóa pavorosa*
>   *n' a escuridade espesa.*
> *En vano a vista con temor n' o escuro*
>   *sin parada vaguea.*

> *Uns tras d' outros istantes silenciosos*
> *pasando van, e silenciosos chegan*
> *outros detrás, n' a eternidá caendo*
> *cal cai ò grau n' a moedora pedra,*
> *sin qu' ò porvir velado ôs mortais ollos*
>   *rompan as pesadas brétemas.*
>
>   *¡Qué triste é a noite, y-o relox qué triste,*
> *s' inquieto ò corpo y-a concencia velan!)* (440)

Memory is a torment; the poet speaks of "infernos of memory" (436). Pleasure recollected taunts her cruelly; grief and remorse inflict pain. All is pervaded by a sense of irrevocable loss, "Why did it end?", "Where did it go?" (444).

Man alone, subject to change *(mudanza)* and extinction, is constantly confronted with reminders of his mortality:

> . . . .
> Men pass, as pass
>   the summer clouds.
> And the stones remain . . . , and when I die,
>   you, cathedral,
> you, dark bulk, ponderous and sad,
> when I am no more, you will still stand.
>
> (. . . .
> *Os homes pasan, tal como pasa*
>   *nube de vran.*
> *Y as pedras quedan . . . , e cand' eu morra,*
>   *ti, catredal;*
> *ti, parda mole, pesada e triste,*
> *cand' eu non sea, t' inda serás.)* (441)

For Rosalía it is nature which presents the cruelest reminder of the brevity of human life:

> . . . .
> Beautiful Nature,
>   eternally the same,
> tell the mortals, tell the fools again
>   that only they perish.
>
> (. . . .
> *Natureza fermosa,*
> *a mesma eternamente,*

dill' os mortáis, de novo os loucos dille
¡qu' eles no máis perecen!) (431)

VIII *Religious Preoccupations*

The awareness of time and eternity, the knowledge of mortality and search for immortality lead to religious or metaphysical preoccupations. In her unbearable suffering, Rosalía seeks, at times, the consolation of religion. The crisis of faith experienced in her early years, as expressed in *La flor*, has not been resolved. She cries out to God but is beset by doubts, and Heaven is silent: "Why, at last, my God,/ at the same time/ heaven and earth fail me?" (*"¿Por qué, en fin, Dios meu,/ a un tempo me faltan/ á terra y ò ceo?"* 433). The Cathedral of Santiago, long a place of solace and inspiration to Rosalía, becomes a place of uneasiness and fright, as she describes in the poem "In the cathedral" ("N'a catredal," 426–28). Reverent and penitent, she enters the temple amid the murmur of prayers, the clamor of organ and bells. The familiar statues are illumined by evening light which enters through the colored glass windows. But the refuge of meditation is not secure; the comfort of prayer does not come. The statues seem to leer and glare at her. For a moment, the sunlight through the colors of the windows seems to dispel this fantasy, but darkness returns, and with it the specters. She prays to her beloved Virgin of Solitude, and flees, afraid.

Abandoned by faith, weary with life, the poet yearns for insensitivity and death. Eternity is a question mark—it may be nothingness or more suffering—but even "not being" (*"no-ser"*) would be preferable: ". . . only death is the remedy/ to cure life." (". . . *soyo é remedio á morte/ para curar d'á vida.*" 541). She sees death as longed for release: "And when the lovely sun/ of April smiles again,/ may it illumine my repose,/ and no longer my suffering." (*"E cando ò sol fermoso/ d' abril torne a sorrir,/ que alume ò meu reposo,/ xa non ò meu sofrir."* 478).

Since death does not come, she is tempted to seek it. Several poems refer to suicide:

. . . .
Why, merciful God,
why do they call it crime
to go in search of reluctant death,
when this life
tires and afflicts one so?

(. . . .
¿Por qué, Dios piadoso,
por qué chaman crime
ir en busca d' a morte que tarda,
cando á un esta vida
lle cansa e lle afrixe?) (447)

The sea, a death symbol, entices her as a lover, inviting her to rest in his cold, mysterious bed, and she would eagerly follow his call: ". . . for if he calls me ceaselessly, I have/ mortal desires to rest in it! . . ." (". . . *que s' él me chama sin parar, ¡eu teño/ un-has ansias mortáis d' apousar n' el! . . .*" 422). A suicide attempt, narrated in first person in "Towers of the West" (*"Torres d' Oeste,"* 544–47), might be either an actual experience or another of Rosalía's dramatizations. The woman who speaks wanders by the sea near the lonely ruins of the towers erected near Padrón in the twelfth century as defense against Viking invaders.[6] Burdened with sorrows, she walks aimlessly, "perhaps fleeing from myself." (545). Grieving for a lost love, solitary and abandoned, she jumps into the current. Rescued and brought back to the world of troubles, she warns others never to go near the towers with a troubled heart.

IX *The muse of sorrow*

The penetrating note of despair in *New Leaves* arises from the futility—or voluntary rejection—of attempts to escape. The shadow remains to haunt and accompany her; the road cannot free her from herself; madness, though experienced, cannot take control of her mind; the "treasure" acquired by guilt vanishes; death cannot be her own choice, she is doomed to live. In spite of its despair and pessimism, the work does not express a negativistic personality, but rather love of beauty and life. The very utilization of the outlet of poetry is a positive gesture. Sorrow is indeed Rosalía's muse, as she stated in her preface, and in *New Leaves* she probes into the creative process of the troubled mind. Each poem shouts defiance against defeat; the words and songs are part of the search for salvation and perfection: " 'Words,' and 'words,' and 'words'!/ The immaculate and pure form of the idea/ where did it remain hidden?" (*"¡'Palabras', e 'palabras', e 'palabras'!/ Da idea á forma inmaculada e pura,/ ¿ónde quedóu velada?"* 423).

Sorrow is the source and substance of her poetry, and lends emo-

tion to what she sees. Sorrow does not arise from things themselves;
things become associated with and expressions for inner reality:

What Is It?

Always a plaintive Ay!, a doubt,
a desire, an anguish, a sorrow . . .
Sometimes it is the glowing star,
and other times a ray of sun;
it is that the leaves fall from the trees,
or that the flowers bloom in the fields,
    and it is the whistling wind,
        it is the cold, it is the warmth . . .
It is not the wind, nor the sun, nor the cold,
        oh no . . . for it is only
the ailing soul, poetic and sensitive
    which everything wounds,
    which everything pains.

(¿Qué Ten?

Sempre un ¡ay!, prañideiro, un-ha duda,
un deseyo, un-ha angustia, un delor . . .
é un-has veces a estrela que brila,
e outras tantas un rayo d' o sol;
é que as follas d' os arbores caen,
e que abrochan n' os campos as frors,
        y é ò vento que zoa,
        y é frío, é ò calor . . .
E n' é o vento, n' é ò sol, nin é ò frío
        non é . . . qu' é tan sô
à alma enferma, poeta e sensibre
    que todo á lastima,
    que todo lle doy.) (482–83)

Rosalía realizes that her poems lack clever artifice and fears that
they are antiesthetic and perhaps not pleasing. She does not sing of
"doves and flowers" (415), and the rhythms are strange. Yet the
poems are inseparable from her inner reality and on this stark,
confessional level they can only reflect her state of soul:

I go searching for honey and coolness
    to refresh my parched lips,
and I know not how nor where, I find
    that which burns and stings.

I go searching for syrups to sweeten
these acrid verses of mine,
and I know not how nor where, they always
acquire a bitter taste.

Heaven and God know well
that I'm not to blame for that;
Alas!, unwillingly it is the fault
of my sick and suffering heart.

(Ando buscando meles e frescura
para os meus labios secos,
y eu non sei com' atopo, nin por ónde,
queimores e amarguexos.

Ando buscando almibres qu' almibaren
estos meus agres versos,
y eu non sei cómo, nin por ónde, sempre
se lles atopa un fero.

Y ò ceo e Dios ben saben
non teño á culpa d' eso;
¡ay!, sin quererlo têna
o lastimado corazón enfermo.) (423)

The theme of sorrow *(dolor)* as muse and unifying element in *New Leaves* might just as well be stated as the theme of love *(amor)*. As Ramón del Valle-Inclán has said, sorrow and love are inseparable in man's tragic state: "Love without pain is a divine comprehension; pain without love, a satanic circle." *("Amor sin dolor es una comprensión divina; Dolor sin amor un círculo de Santanás.")*[7] In *Follas novas* the one is directly proportionate to the other; the intensity of pain and loss are commensurate to the love and joy she has felt and experienced. "I hate you, green fields!" she cries out, "And you, gentle hills, I hate you!" Then she concludes: "Because I loved you greatly/ is why I hate you so!" *("¡Porque vos améi tanto/ é porque así vos odio!"* 518).

X Summation: The Tragic Sense.

Rosalía's search for self has probed to universal depths. The themes which preoccupy her on a personal level come to express the eternal preoccupations of mankind which center around the meaning of existence. The Muse of Sorrow, she states in her foreword, is the "muse of our times" (410). Therefore, her own sorrow is not exclusively hers and this extremely intimate series of poems is indeed very much an expression of its own times and succeeding ones. Rosalía touches upon the central theme of man's yearning for immortality in the face of his mortality; the dilemma of body and spirit, heart and mind; the desire to transcend reason and to know absolutely. This timeless theme will come into sharp focus in the years immediately following 1900. Unamuno will enunciate it philosophically as "the tragic sense of life" ("*el sentimiento trágico de la vida*"); Fernando Pessoa will call it "the dolorous enigma of life" ("*o doloroso enigma da vida*"); and Rubén Darío will express it succinctly in his brief poem "Fate" ("*Lo fatal*"). It embraces what it is to be human and became the pivotal concern of the modern poets—the anguished expression of an introspective age where reason and intuition deadlocked and faith became problematic. Although *New Leaves* (1880) preceded the cited statements of Unamuno, Pessoa, and Darío by some twenty years, it is useless to speak of influence. Antecedents could be found as far back as man gave thought to his being and expressed his feelings. It is rather a case of universal human experience and the spirit of the age. Each one lived it alone, and thereby coincided with the others.

Follas novas, belying the title's symbolic suggestion, ends on a suspended note of suffering.

CHAPTER 7

En las orillas del Sar
(On the Banks of the River Sar)

I *Background*

THE collection of poetry *En las orillas del Sar (On the Banks of the River Sar)*, 1884, is Rosalía's last book of poetry and last published work. Between the publication of *Follas novas (New Leaves)* in 1880, and the appearance of *The Sar*, she had published a novel, *El primer loco (The First Madman)*, in 1881, and a long article, "Padrón y las inundaciones" ("Padrón and the Floods"), which was serialized in the periodical *La Ilustración Gallega y Asturiana* (Madrid), also in 1881. Her literary career begins and closes with poetry. *The Sar* is, like *New Leaves*, an accumulation of poems written over several years' time, mostly between 1878 and 1884, so that the two volumes chronologically overlap somewhat. A number of the poems in *The Sar* appeared separately in periodicals, such as *La Nación Española* of Buenos Aires, before their publication as a collection.

The second and best known edition was organized by Murguía. The only introduction is a brief poem which offers the compositions to the reader as "simple and brief songs" ("*fáciles y breves . . . canciones*") and "short, but fervent prayers" ("*cortas, pero fervientes oraciones*"). Since this edition of 1909 was posthumous, it is not known if this prefatory poem would have expressed Rosalía's intention, but it seems appropriate.

Murguía wrote a preface for the second edition, which contains biographical information and critical judgments from a later perspective—twenty-four years after Rosalía's death and already into the twentieth century, when her contributions were being recognized and evaluated with a new esthetic spirit. Murguía, always defender and proponent of his wife's work, recalls the discouraging indifference it met in her life, except for the success and diffusion of *Cantares*. He remarks on her renovation of Galician as a literary language (567), and the passionate sincerity that always inspired her (558). Calling her a "modern poet" (558), he notes the importance of her metrical innovations, which evoked negative reactions in her own day, but which at the time of Murguía's preface (i.e. post-Modernism) were being recognized as significant, earning for Rosalía the title of "precursor" (559–60).

II *Language*

Orillas is written in Castilian. Rosalía had freed herself from the sense of obligation to use Galician, as she had freed herself from adherence to *costumbrismo,* or local and popular themes. In this final work, she writes in the literary language of Spain, addressing herself to the wider audience of the cultured Spanish-speaking world. The Castilian she commands is a conscious, poetic language, dignified and literary. It is natural, but not colloquial, a more formal artistic medium in keeping with the profound and universal message it contains.

More accessible to Spanish readers and students of literature, *The Sar* is Rosalía's most widely known work. The attention is well placed, since it represents a point of plentitude. Rosalía lived only forty-eight years, yet her work was mature, with a wealth of life experience condensed into that short span. *The Sar* has led those who became acquainted with her through its pages to explore and give due attention to her other works. In spite of her disavowal of things Galician in her heated letter to Murguía of 1881, this last work has brought the author, and through her Galicia, to a wider appreciation than *Cantares* ever did.

III *Organization and Forms*

The Sar, in contrast to the rather hasty assemblage of *New Leaves,* was selected and arranged with care and forethought. Typically for Rosalía, however, organization and arrangement are not strict, although there is more consistency and homogeneity.

The metric devices in *Orillas* are not new, most having appeared in the previous collection, but they have evolved and matured as the adequate vessel for the more serene and detached mood of the poems. Detectable differences in rhythm and syntax are due to the varying exigencies and possibilities of Castilian. She continues to employ unusual combinations of lines and broken rhythms. There is a noticeable tendency to longer lines—slow, meditative, almost proselike. She frequently employs the twelve- and fourteen-syllable lines already seen in *Follas*, and some even longer, of sixteen and eighteen syllables. For the more song-like compositions, the fluid traditional meters of the *romance* (eight syllables) and the *silva* (seven and eleven syllables) are used. Rhyme is predominantly assonant, in flexible combinations, although there is a tendency to more use of consonant rhyme, and some free verse occurs. Syntax has come 180 degrees from the imitation of oral patterns in *Cantares;* sentence arrangement now obeys the convoluted order of artistic design. The result is a sensitive, flexible, and highly developed poetic instrument.

In this volume, as in its predecessor, content seeks form and form enhances content. In this respect, Rosalía's proximity to the modern poets is evident, as César Barja notes: "She is a very modern poet, the most modern of Spanish poets of the nineteenth century because never did her technique of versification dominate poetry. True modern poetry, whose law may be said to consist of the total subordination of verse to poetry, to inner rhythm, to music, begins with Rosalía de Castro. . . ."[1]

IV *Comparison with* Follas novas (New Leaves)

There is great continuity between *Follas novas* and *En las orillas del Sar.* Like movements of a musical composition, they are linked by themes, varied by tempo and interpretations. *The Sar* grows out of the previous work, but the subtle yet significant change in the inward structure of the latter makes it impossible to outline them in exactly the same way.

The Sar represents further maturation of style and ideas. It is permeated with trouble and sorrow, yet is more restrained, with flashes of hope. There is an intellectual and philosophical detachment, a relinquishing of life, a quiet preparation to die. All her life Rosalía had felt close to death, as evidenced by her own statements and those of Murguía and others, as well as by expressions of the theme in her poetry. In *La flor* and *New Leaves*, her suffering of life is so unbearable that she longs and pleads for death and talks of suicide. At the time she sent *The Sar* to press, she knew she was dying. In death's very presence, she confronts it calmly, with a final tribute to life she has loved so intensely, a final query as to human destiny, and that dignified acceptance which the Spanish so admire as "the good death" *("el buen morir")*—to have finished one's life, to have filled it to the utmost, to die bravely.

To pursue the psychological interpretation of her work applied to *New Leaves* in Chapter 6, there has been an evolution in her psychic state. The contents of both are subjective, seeking their expression metaphorically and symbolically, but a more intellectual process can be discerned in *The Sar*. It is as though, having passed through the "dark night" of *Follas*, the poet comes "into the light once more" (as the mystics and Dante describe it). The external world, consciously perceived reality, is not separate and hostile, but fused with her being. She has taken it into herself as a dream, and she joins with it as part of the natural cosmic process. There is no sudden, miraculous solution, but a perceptible direction toward wholeness. Through art, which has always been her outlet, she comes closer to surmounting her suffering. The words of Henry Miller, with reference to Anaïs Nin, fit Rosalía's experience as well:

The therapeutic aspect of art is then, in this higher state of consciousness, seen to be the religious or metaphysical element. The work which was begun as a refuge and escape from the terrors of reality leads the author back into life, not *adapted* to the reality about, but *superior* to it, as one capable of recreating it in accordance with his own needs. He sees that it was not life but himself from which he had been fleeing, and that the life which had heretofore been insupportable was merely the projection of his own fantasies. It is true that the new life is also a projection of the individual's own fantasies but they are invested now with a sense of real power; they spring not from dissociation but from integration. . . .[2]

The stylistic elements of *The Sar*, as compared to *New Leaves*, offer less indication of turbulence and confusion. The rhythms are more ordered, the diction more controlled. Colors are muted, or reduced to shades of light and dark, as in the earlier collection, but with less darkness and more luminosity. The themes from *New Leaves* continued in *Orillas* may modulate to greater intensity or diminish in importance, while characteristic images and symbols also evolve in their significance, as will be discussed below.

V   Dolor *and Other Themes*

As in the preceding volume, *dolor* is the all-pervasive theme of *The Sar*, a sorrow and pain accepted now as a permanent part of the meaning of life:

He who weeps goes not alone,
do not dry up, I beg you!, tears of mine;
one grief satisfies the soul;
never, never will happiness suffice.

Plaything of destiny, humble straw,
I wandered sad and lost;
but with me I had everything:
I had my sorrow for companion.

(No va solo el que llora,
no os sequéis, ¡por piedad!, lágrimas mías;
basta un pesar del alma;
jamás, jamás le bastará una dicha.

Juguete del destino, arista humilde,
rodé triste y perdida;
pero conmigo lo llevaba todo:
llevaba mi dolor por compañía.) (653)

Galicia is less often specifically mentioned in *Orillas*. Two poems of topical interest refer to the cutting of oak trees, which Rosalía considers tragically destructive (588–91; 593–97). Her vehement protest reveals a remarkably contemporary sense of ecology. There is an occasional recurrence of the theme of emigration, linked to her own spiritual exile. Galicia has become symbolic of the poet's withdrawal into self, her physical and spiritual estrangement from the vitality and bustle of the world. The folk element has almost entirely disappeared.

Galicia is, nonetheless, constantly present in the nature the poems reflect and incorporate. *The Sar* contains some of the most beautiful nature poetry in Spanish literature, wherein nature is described not for its own sake, but forms the whole fabric of imagery. It is the source of recognizable symbols through which inner realities are communicated. Rosalía's lifelong love and close observation of nature and intimate communion with it are evident. It is Galician nature, reduced geographically to the features of her particular locale—yet it captures the spirit of the whole region and thereby a facet of the soul of Spain.

Nature images are used in a traditional sense, expressing the timeless human truth of the eternal involvement of nature with human life and destiny. The rotation of the seasons; water in its various forms of rain, fog, snow, streams, and the sea; trees, flowers,

and paths; all have the expected associations. The images are not
trite, however, for they have the original freshness of lived experience, while evoking sympathetic recognition in the reader of all
times and places by touching on universal experience. The result is
that profound and complex themes are uttered in a limpid and
accessible idiom.

In many of the poems, the fusion of outer and inner worlds, noted
previously in *Follas*, becomes a clearly identifiable process. It is the
process which Fernando Pessoa describes: "Every state of soul is a
landscape." *("Todo o estado de alma é uma paisagem.")* Hence man
is conscious, at one and the same time, of two landscapes, the
exterior one and the spiritual one. "Therefore art which attempts to
represent reality will have to do so by means of a simultaneous
representation of the interior landscape and the exterior landscape.
It will have to try to render an intersection of two landscapes. . . ."
*("De maneira que a arte que queira representar bem a realidade terá
de a dar através duma representação simultânea da paisagem interior e da paisagem exterior. Resulta que terá de tentar dar uma
intersecção de duas paisagens. . . .")*[3]
Carlos Bousoño, in his discussion of the poetry of Antonio
Machado, employs the term "bisemic symbols" for objects which
retain their intrinsic natural qualities while representing spiritual
values.[4] The title "On the Banks of the River Sar" is an illustration of
the "bisemic" nature of Rosalía's nature symbols. The Sar is the
beloved river of her homeland, and also signifies the flowing of life
toward the unknown; its banks are the brink of destiny:

> O earth, then as now, ever fecund and beautiful!
> Seeing how sadly our fatal star gleams
>   on the banks of the Sar,
> as I expire, I feel the devouring thirst,
> never quenched, which chokes all feelings,
> and the hunger for justice, which weakens and destroys
> while the wind of the angry tempest
>   snatches away our cries. . . .

> *(¡Oh tierra, antes y ahora, siempre fecunda y bella!*
> *Viendo cuán triste brilla nuestra fatal estrella,*
> *   del Sar cabe la orilla,*
> *al acabarme, siento la sed devoradora*
> *y jamás apagada que ahoga el sentimiento,*

y el hambre de justicia, que abate y que anonada
cuando nuestros clamores los arrebata el viento
de tempestad airada. . . .) (574–75)

Another example of the "bisemic" symbol and the "intersection of two landscapes" is the poem "White road, old road" ("*Camino blanco, viejo camino*," 603–604), which proceeds from the description of a familiar country road to the symbolic implications of the "long journey of life." The weary traveler who is the poet herself now seeks the more desolate reaches, apart from the busy thoroughfare.[5]

Once again, the poet dwells upon the more tragic aspects of love in *The Sar*. A few narrative-dramatic portrayals of guilty and fatal love are included, such as "Margarita" (582–84), where the theme is projected through the mask of her characters. Love is seen as passion, madness, temptation, poison, the source of regret and sorrow. Several compositions deal with the untimely resurgence of passion in the old, when it is hopeless and incongruous, yet real and intense nonetheless. One of the most poignant expressions of this autumnal love is "The Song which the Old Man Heard in his Dreams" ("*La canción que oyó en sueños el viejo*" 608–609).

In a more subjective vein, without the mask of *personae*, she links love with the exuberant aspects of nature—spring, flowers, leaves—which now to her are only memories:

. . . .
    It passed, the summer passed rapidly, as passes
a happy feverish dream of love,
and now dry leaves on naked branches,
all faded, tremble, awaiting death. . . .

(. . . .
    Pasó, pasó el verano rápido, como pasa
un venturoso sueño de amor en la fiebre,
y ya secas las hojas en las ramas desnudas,
tiemblan descoloridas esperando la muerte. . . .) (604)

The memories still have power to wound; the passions still smolder; life and love are synonymous:

    Now my passions sleep soundly in their tomb
        the sleep of nothingness;

is it, then, madness of the suffering spirit,
or a worm which gnaws upon my being?
I only know it is a pleasure which gives pain,
a sorrow which, tormenting, causes pleasure:
flame which takes its nourishment from life,
but without which life itself would die.

(*Ya duermen en su tumba las pasiones*
   el sueño de la nada;
¿es, pues, locura del doliente espíritu,
o gusano que llevo en mis entrañas?
Yo sólo sé que es un placer que duele,
que es un dolor que atormentando halaga:
llama que de la vida se alimenta,
mas sin la cual la vida se apagara.) (592)

VI   *Evolution of Images and Symbols*

Some of the basic images and symbols of *New Leaves* (discussed
in Chapter 6), while retaining something of their original connota-
tions, have evolved significantly in *The Sar* in response to the
change in psychic state which has occurred.

The analogy between physical sensations and sufferings of the
soul is used much as seen earlier. Hunger, thirst, cold, weariness,
and sickness convey yearnings of the spirit. One example will
suffice: "Do not censure the one who, already drunk, hastens to
drink with renewed desire;/ his eternal thirst is what leads him to
the burning fountain,/ to drink the more, the more he drinks." ("*No
maldigáis del que, ya ebrio, corre a beber con nuevo afán;/ su eterna
sed es quien le lleva hacia la fuente abasadora,/ cuanto más bebe, a
beber más.*" 609).

The shadow *(sombra)* is a frequently occurring image in *The Sar*,
but its meaning is now more positive than the projection of the
troubled specter of the psyche it represented in *New Leaves*. In the
later work, it is sometimes the penumbra of shade, cool refuge for
the soul which seeks peace and darkness; or it may represent the
obverse of reality—the reflected shadows of birds on the water.
Shadow and other equivalent terms, such as *tinieblas*, also represent the poet's inner world, the tenebrous realm of illusion and
dream to which she has withdrawn: "—Leave me alone, and forgotten, and free:/ I want to wander at will in the shadows;/ my dearest

illusion/ only there, sweetly and without shame, kisses me." ("—
Dejadme solo, y olvidado, y libre:/ quiero errante vagar en las tinie-
blas;/ mi ilusión más querida/ sólo allí dulce y sin rubor me besa."
581).

Often shadows or phantoms represent memory, evocations from
the past, lost dreams or illusions. The rough and weary road of life
"is still filled with the white phantoms/ we adored in other times."
("... *lleno aún de las blancas fantasmas/ que en otro tiempo*
adoramos." 573). In these manifestations, the shadow is beautiful
and comforting. It can also mean doubt and sadness:

> . . . .
> When, in the fearful deep darkness
> of an atheistic soul
> there shines a ray of faith, doubt comes
> and extends over it a giant shadow.

> (. . . .
> *Cuando de un alma atea*
> *en la profunda oscuridad medrosa*
> *brilla un rayo de fe, viene la duda*
> *y sobre él tiende su gigante sombra.)* (585)

At times the shadow suggests restlessness, the pursuit of vague,
impossible illusions:

> A mournful shadow, indefinable and vague
> as uncertainty, always goes before my eyes,
> pursuing another vague shadow which flees from it,
>   running ceaselessly.
> I know not their destiny . . .; but somehow I fear,
>   seeing their mortal anguish,
> that they can never stop, nor will they ever meet.

> *(Una sombra tristísima, indefinible y vaga*
> *como lo incierto, siempre ante mis ojos va.*
> *tras de otra vaga sombra que sin cesar la huye,*
>   *corriendo sin cesar.*
> *Ignoro su destino . . .; mas no sé por qué temo*
>   *al ver su ansia mortal,*
> *que ni han de parar nunca, ni encontrarse jamás.)* (607)

The terrifying aspects of the shadow which so characterized earlier poems in the Galician predecessor—fear, misfortune, remorse, and the like—seem to disappear in the final collection in Castilian.

Nature images (springs, winter, the desert, the road) occur frequently in *Follas*, and they have much the same thematic associations in *The Sar*. However, in the latter their symbolic use has become more definitive and there has been a change toward more positive values. The streams and springs in *New Leaves* were often forbidden or poisonous, representing furtive love or abandoned hope. In *Orillas* they gush forth again, "serene and pure." The springs of life are now inaccessible to the poet, but she can envision other springs which beckon:

> . . . .
> But no matter! In the distance another stream murmurs
> where humble violets perfume the air.

> . . . .
> The thirsty traveler passing by on the road
> moistens his lips in the serene liquid
> of the stream, which the tree shades with its boughs,
> and blissful, forgets the spring which has dried.

> . . . .
> *¡Mas no importa! A lo lejos otro arroyo murmura*
> *donde humildes violetas al espacio perfuman.*

> . . . .
> *El sediento viajero que el camino atraviesa*
> *humedece los labios en la linfa serena*
> *del arroyo, que el árbol con sus ramas sombrea,*
> *y dichoso se olvida de la fuente ya seca.)* (599)

Winter now becomes one of the most predominant nature images. It retains the earlier implications of age, sterility, and death, and there is still the bitter awareness of the contrast between the winter of life and the vigor and abundance of nature. The poet finds summer ironically sad and unendurable, with its cruel reminders of her lost youth (580). More and more she seeks refuge in winter, which is in harmony with her soul, and she delights in the "discordant harmony" of its storms (600). She calls it "friend," "companion," and "lover"; it comes to represent solace and peace.

Before, winter represented finality and quiet despair. Now, in *The Sar*, winter is not the end of the year, but the beginning, a prelude to spring. The poet cherishes the dream that the winter of life may also be a prelude:

> . . . .
> Oh winter my friend!
> you are a thousand times welcome,
> my somber and stern companion;
> are you not perchance the joyous precursor
> of gentle May and smiling April?
>
> Ah! if only the sad wintertime of life
> as you are of the flowers and the zephyrs,
> were also precursor of the lovely
> and eternal springtime of my dreams!
>
> (. . . .
> *¡Oh mi amigo el invierno!,*
> *mil y mil veces bien venido seas,*
> *mi sombrío y adusto compañero;*
> *¿no eres acaso el precursor dichoso*
> *del tibio mayo y del abril risueño?*
>
> *¡Ah!, si el invierno triste de la vida,*
> *como tú de las flores y los céfiros,*
> *también precursor fuera de la hermosa*
> *y eterna primavera de mis sueños!*) (600)

The word *desierto* in Spanish can be both the noun "desert" and the adjective "deserted." It contains, therefore, a multitude of suggestions—arid, barren, empty space; solitude, desolation, sterility; sunlight, purity, and spirituality. The desert in *New Leaves* represented the ugly and the despicable, being a landscape most alien to a Galician. Symbolically it was associated with darkness, barrenness, and suffering. These implications persist in the Castilian poems, but there appears a more positive note as well. It comes to represent not the desert in the midst of life—sterility surrounded by vitality and fecundity—but rather the desert at the end of life, a realm beyond the suffering of the flesh, illumined by "another light more vivid than that of the golden sun" ("*otra luz más viva que la del sol dorado,*" 620). There man, the tragic hero, stripped of joy and hope, but calm and serene, stands alone with his destiny. The road of life, as it nears its end, having passed by the flowers, fields, trees, and streams, now leads on into the desert, a " 'realm of abstraction'. . . outside the realm of existence,"[6] open, pure, and luminous.

The evolution of the symbol of the road strikingly reveals the change between the dark and troubled soul-state of *New Leaves* and the progress toward harmony and individuation or self-fulfillment manifested in *The Sar*. The road of the earlier volume, as illustrated in the poem "From here I see a road" ("*Dend' aquí vexo un camino*," 538), is closed as an avenue of escape. The poet longs to follow and lose herself, but is rooted to her suffering and realizes the futility of attempting to flee from self. The road of *The Sar* leads on into infinity and beckons the poet, a weary pilgrim unconcerned with wordly pursuits, to follow. She takes with her, not dark specters, but the "white phantoms" of memory:

> . . . .
> The white and deserted way,
>   among the leafy hedges
> and the woods and brooks which border
> its edges, with appealing mystery
> seems to attract me, and invite me
> to follow its endless line.
>
> Let us go on, then, for the old road
>   will come to meet our steps,
> although sad, uneven and deserted,
>   and like ourselves changed,
> it is still filled with the white phantoms
>   we adored in other times.
>
> (. . . .
> *Blanca y desierta la vía,*
>   *entre los frondosos setos*
> *y los bosques y arroyos que bordan*
> *sus orillas, con grato misterio*
> *atraerme parece, y brindarme*
> *a que se siga su línea sin término.*
>
> *Bajemos, pues, que el camino*
>   *antiguo nos saldrá al paso,*
> *aunque triste, escabroso y desierto,*
>   *y cual nosotros cambiado,*
> *lleno aún de las blancas fantasmas*
>   *que en otro tiempo adoramous*). (573)[7]

VII   *Time and Dream States*

The theme of time assumes greater preponderance. Man's sense
of temporality is synonymous with his awareness of his own finiteness contrasted with the relative permanence of the world around
him and his notion of eternity. This temporal sense is a function of
his psychic processes, a sixth sense and a fourth dimension. In those
of intellectual-metaphysical bent, it is a source of anguish. Rosalía's
life is now nearing its end; the present is tenuous, the future an
enigma. "Life" itself is in the past—relived in the present as memory. She experiences time in its linear flow—one-way and irreversi-
ble, and also in its vertical dimension—the inner confusion of memory of lived moments, immediate awareness, and imagined realities
called dreams.

External reality is perceived by the poet at a distance. Abundant
adverbs express this separation between her inner reality and the
actual reality which surrounds her: "from afar," "no longer," "at a
distance," "from my window." Her mortal life is now in the past, but
fuses with the present through the evocation of memories. Verbs in
past and present tenses mingle in the same thought: "I hear the
sonorous peal which used to come then/ to my bed to call me . . ."
(*"Oigo el toque sonoro que entonces/ a mi lecho a llamarme venía
. . ."* 572). Reality is an echo of itself: "Like a lost echo, like a
friendly voice/ which rings lovingly, the familiar creak of the lazy
cart/ travels on wings of wind . . ." (*"Como un eco perdido, como un
amigo acento/ que suena cariñoso, el familiar chirrido del carro
perezoso/ corre en alas del viento . . ."* 573).

Almost every image in *The Sar* relates in some way to this sense of
time. The greenness and flowers of living nature suggest growth,
fecundity, and renewal. Day and night and the seasons of the year
correspond to the ages of man. Water and its flow are time's passing;
the sea is accumulation—or cessation—of time. Rosalía has come in
her own life experience to the discovery of Heraclitus, that all is
eternally change. The water flows, but it is never the same water;
the leaves and flowers appear each spring, but they are not the same
ones. Man pursues his relentless, brief, forward trajectory, aware of
the change while retaining through memory his own constancy. The
mind asks the eternal question: *Ubi sunt?*—Where have they gone?:

. . . .
Times that were, tears and laughter,

black torments and gentle lies,
alas!, where did they leave their trace,
where, oh soul of mine?

(. . . .
    Tiempos que fueron, llantos y risas,
    negros tormentos, dulces mentiras,
    ¡ay!, ¿en dónde su rastro dejaron,
        en dónde, alma mía?) (656)

The road, more than any other symbol, represents the linear,
chronological journey of the individual life. It has passed through
forests and flowers, ardent summer and abundant autumn. Now it
leads through the arid waste. The poet can only walk forward, accompanied by experiences from the past which are recreated
through memory when evoked by sounds or other sensations. The
experiences relived, like the water and flowers she sees and the
music she hears, are the same yet different. The emotion they produce is constant—a painful sense of loss. Songs from other times
bring back haunting images of lost illusions and the poet cries out: "I
beg you, do not sing to me those songs/ which I heard in other
times!" ("*¡Por Dios, no me cantéis esas canciones/ que en otro tiempo
oía!*" 635). Happiness is gone, memory is suffering: "Why has
Heaven endowed me with such a vivid and faithful memory?" ("*¿Por
qué tan cerca/ tan fiel memoria me ha dado el Cielo?*" 592).

The poet's keen awareness of mortal time and her own personal
time gives rise to pondering on what might be called "cosmic" time:

A firefly glimmers in the moss
and a star is twinkling up on high;
abyss above, and in the depths, abyss:
what, after all, will end and what remain? . . .

Una luciérnaga entre el musgo brilla
y un astro en las alturas centellea;
abismo arriba, y en el fondo, abismo:
¿qué es al fin lo que acaba y lo que queda? . . . (577)

Man's concern for his own finiteness is projected toward the immense scope of the universe, with implications of a consciousness of
matter: "But who can know if, while they march toward their des-
tiny/ the stars, like man, dream of being eternal?" ("*¿Mas quién sabe*

En las orillas del Sar *(On the Banks of the River Sar)* 91

si en tanto hacia su fin caminan?/ ¡Como el hombre, los astros con ser eternos sueñan!" 606).

It is man's consciousness which gives him his sense of time, and can be his defense against it. If reality of here and now does not belong to the poet, but is only a reflection or an echo of memories which haunt but cannot be recaptured, wherein lies reality? Ultimately, it is subjective; external stimuli evoke subjective reactions and are transmuted into psychic realities:

> A quiet river, a narrow path,
> a solitary field and a grove of pines,
> and the old bridge, rustic and simple,
> completing such welcome solitude.
>
> What is solitude? To fill the world
> a single thought at times suffices.
> Therefore, today, replete with beauty, you find
> the bridge, the river and the lonely grove.
>
> It is not the cloud nor the flower which enamors,
> it is you, oh heart, sad or joyful,
> arbiter of sorrow or of pleasure,
> who dries the sea and makes habitable the pole.

> *(Un manso río, una vereda estrecha,*
> *un campo solitario y un pinar,*
> *y el viejo puente, rústico y sencillo,*
> *completando tan grata soledad.*
>
> *¿Qué es soledad? Para llenar el mundo*
> *basta a veces un solo pensamiento.*
> *Por eso hoy, hartos de belleza, encuentras*
> *el puente, el río, y el pinar desierto.*
>
> *No son nube ni flor los que enamoran,*
> *eres tú, corazón, triste o dichoso,*
> *ya del dolor y del placer el árbitro,*
> *quien seca el mar y hace habitable el polo.)* (580–81)

Although afflicted by the anguish of time's passage and the fear of her own extinction, the poet finds a realm where time and natural laws have no power—the world of dreams. The dream is a frequently recurring word throughout *Orillas*. It has none of the nightmarish qualities which it often had in *Follas*—dark, fearful stirrings of the unconscious and disturbing visions and fantasies.

Dream in *Orillas* is the creative faculty of the mind, the ultrareality
of a personal interpretation of the world. In her refuge of dreams,
Rosalía again brings to mind the Generation of 1898 and the theme
of *sueño* or *ensueño* so prevalent in Unamuno, Antonio Machado,
and Azorín. Faced with the disillusionments of the world and with
the inevitable fate of mortality, the mind builds other realities:

> . . . .
> It matters not that dreams be lies,
>   since, after all, it is true
> that he who dies dreaming is fortunate,
>   unhappy, he who lives without dreams. . . .
>
> (. . . .
> *No importa que los sueños sean mentira,*
>   *ya que, al cabo, es verdad*
> *que es venturoso el que soñando muere,*
>   *infeliz el que vive sin soñar. . . .*) (579)

The dream is closely related to other projections of idealized
reality—hope, happiness, beauty, and illusion. It leads the poet on
and prevents her from succumbing to resignation or despair: "But
he knows you exist and are not a vain dream,/ beauty without name,
perfect and unique . . ." (*"Pero sabe que existes y no eres vano
sueño,/ hermosura sin nombre, pero perfecta y única . . ."* 621). The
poet is "condemned to dream" (611). The dream represents freedom
from the rational, the refusal to accept the miserable limitations of
man, hence it is "madness" *(locura)*. Rosalía often refers to herself as
"la loca," which is synonymous with dreamer or poet. In one of her
most serenely beautiful poems, "They say that plants do not speak"
(*"Dicen que no hablan las plantas"*), she asserts that indeed they do
speak to her, for they murmur: "—There goes the madwoman,
dreaming/ of the eternal spring of life and fields . . ." (*"—Ahí va la
loca, soñando/ con la eterna primavera de la vida y de los campos
. . ."* 627). They remind her that soon the frost will cover her hair,
as it will soon cover the fields. The poet replies:

> "—There are white hairs on my head;
> there is frost on the fields;
> but I go on dreaming, poor incurable somnambulist,
> of the eternal spring of now fading life
> and the perennial freshness of fields and of souls,
> though fields may parch and souls may wither.

Stars and fountains and flowers!,
do not murmur at my dreams;
without them, how can I admire you,
nor how can I live without them?

("—Hay canas en mi cabeza; hay en los prados escarcha;
mas yo prosigo soñando, pobre, incurable somnámbula,
con la eterna primavera de la vida que se apaga
y la perenne frescura de los campos y las almas,
aunque los unos se agostan y aunque las otras se abrasan.

¡Astros y fuentes y flores!, no murmuréis de mis sueños;
sin ellos, ¿cómo admiraros ni cómo vivir sin ellos?") (627)

VIII *Poetry*

Poetry is, in essence, the work of the dreamer who dares to
understand, interpret, and re-form reality in accord with the inner
vision. For Rosalía, the secret of poetry lies in the capacity to
dream. Her attitudes toward poetry are expressed throughout *The
Sar.* They do not deviate essentially from the concepts expressed
previously, but now find their definitive expression as she probes
the mystery of the subjective drama and the creative process.

A long poem, "Those who through their tears" ("*Los que a través
de sus lágrimas,*" 629–33), traces Rosalía's poetic trajectory, which is
at the same time her struggle for liberation and authenticity. The
public wishes to hear no sad songs, and urges the poet to speak in
"facile verses" about hope, not disillusionment. Resolutely, the poet
puts aside her grief and shoos away the "black-winged thoughts" in
order to pursue those with white wings. She sings of happier
themes—love and youth. Applause rings out and she is acclaimed by
all. Then she returns to "the desolate world of former loves" (633),
and incurs the scorn of the crowds, which briefly wounds her, but
she defies criticism and remains true to herself:

And I said to my heart: "If your passion is not vain
and in you the founts of love and sentiment o'erflow,
fountains in which the poet quenches his divine thirst,
be you my muse and let us sing, without asking the people
if they love happy ballads or sorrowful sighs,
or if they prefer the rising sun or seek the one which declines."

> *(Y a mi corazón le dije: "Si no es vano tu ardimiento*
> *y en ti el manantial rebosa del amor y el sentimiento,*
> *fuentes en donde el poeta apaga su sed divina,*
> *sé tú mi musa y cantemos sin preguntarle a las gentes*
> *si aman las alegres trovas o los suspiros dolientes,*
> *si gustan del sol que nace o buscan al que declina.")* (633)

The correspondence between the poem and her own career is apparent. Her first poetic expressions in *La flor* are introspective and tragic in tone. Although she matures in wisdom and artistry, she basically remains true to that. The happy themes, public acclaim, and brief subjugation to the whims of popularity and glory can be related to *Cantares gallegos*, which she subsequently renounced with the trace of bitterness evidenced in the prologue to *New Leaves* and the letter to Murguía. With *New Leaves* she renews her loyalty to "the muse of sadness" and withdraws to the shadowy inner world. *The Sar* offers explicit and implicit disregard for the "hundred-armed monster" of public acclaim (611). Glory is ephemeral:

> . . . .
> I prefer to that flash of an instant
> the mournful solitude in which I battle,
> where never enters to perturb my spirit
> the vain murmur of applause.

> (. . . .
> *Yo prefiero de ese brillo de un instante*
> *la triste soledad donde batallo,*
> *y adonde nunca a perturbar mi espíritu*
> *llega el vano rumor de los aplausos.)* (650)

The words "solitude" and "battle" characterize Rosalía's view of the poet and his art. The poet engages in a lonely and ceaseless struggle to express all of life and to attempt the ineffable. Knowing, with a nod to the scientific enthusiasm of her times, that Science, Progress, and Fame are inevitable, but futile, human pursuits, the poet out of "vice, passion, or, perhaps sickness of soul" continues to cast his bitter drops into the boundless sea. Part of nature that he is, he sings because he must (649–50). Poetry is not written for any self-interested purpose, but arises from the dolorous inner struggle for identity and meaning:

They thought that he was idle
in his narrow prison
and never could the one
be idle who, firm in the breach,
in desperate warfare
struggles against himself.

They thought he was alone,
and yet alone never was
the creator of phantoms
who sees always in the real
the false, and in his visions,
the image of the truth.

(Pensaban que estaba ocioso
en sus prisiones estrechas
y nunca estarlo ha podido
quien, firme al pie de la brecha,
en guerra desesperada,
contra sí mismo pelea.

Pensaban que estaba solo,
y no lo estuvo jamás
el forjador de fantasmas
que ve siempre en lo real
lo falso, y en sus visiones,
la imagen de la verdad. 634)

In *The Sar* the struggle with self has surmounted its destructiveness; the "creator of phantoms" spiritualizes reality and realizes dreams, and poetry becomes the avenue to a higher state of consciousness.

IX   *Death and Religion*

The Sar is a book preoccupied with death, and this preoccupation leads to meditation on the mystery of what comes after it. The poet knows she is dying; her lifelong premonitions of early death are now a certainty. The note of weariness and longing for release is dominant. She is the "weary pilgrim" desirous of insensibility and peace, now mature enough not to hasten death but to await its proper hour. She stands calmly "on the banks," facing her destiny. Extenuated by physical and spiritual suffering, she would welcome death: "the body inclines toward repose,/ and the soul toward eternity." ("*el cuerpo tiende al reposo,/ el alma tiende a lo eterno.*" 586). However,

Orillas is by no means an expression of a passive acceptance of death; the intensity of its power lies in the dramatic conflict between the recognition of inevitable fate and the reluctance to relinquish all she has loved. She longs to know what it all means and yet is terrified of the "undiscovered country" beyond. Rosalía does not approach death like a saint or a mystic. The awareness of its nearness only intensifies her love for life, its beauties and its pleasures. Death is accepted, for it is the way of all nature and will mean repose for the weary clay. The spirit, freed, may find the answer. Will it be a dream? Or nothingness? Perhaps, after all, the soul will drink at the spring of the seraphim (584).

Rosalía's religious attitude might be summed up in the question, "Who knows?" ("*¿Quién sabe?*"). She has pondered with anguish and deep penetration the "dolorous enigma" of man—his mortality and quest for eternity. Even in what she knows to be her final days, there is no return to faith, though she yearns for it: "Happy the one who hopes/ after this life to find a better one!" ("*¡Dichoso aquel que espera/ tras de esta vida hallarse en mejor vida!*" 654). Her religion has become, like Unamuno's, search and doubt, and she feels something very like his "*anhelo vital,*" or the longing for eternity while retaining individual consciousness. She does not seek a union with the Absolute, for that would mean extinction of identity: "You can never erase from the human soul/ . . . that pride of the being which resists/ losing a single atom of itself." ("*No borraréis jamás del alma humana/ . . . el orgullo del ser que se resiste/ a perder de su ser un solo átomo.*" 635). Even in the poems which might appear to be the most religious in a traditional sense, the key expressions "I seek," "I hope," "I yearn," indicate lack of certainty. Her penetrating intellectual scrutiny will not let her be contained in conventional molds, nor believe implicitly, yet she feels strongly that the human spirit does not perish:

> . . . .
> Only the human spirit, rolling out
> of its orbit to sad and desolate worlds,
> neither succumbs nor dies: for the strong hammer
> of sorrow, which crushes and shatters
> mortal dust and clay, cannot break it, nor loosen
> the mysterious ties which bind it to eternity. . . .
>
> (. . . .
> *Sólo el humano espíritu, al rodar desquiciado*

desde su órbita a mundos tristes y desolados,
ni sucumbe ni muere: que del dolor el mazo
fuerte, que abate el polvo y que quebranta el barro
mortal, romper no puede, ni desatar los lazos
que con lo eterno le unen por misterioso arcano. . . .) (620)

X Art, Poetry, God

These words and their placement in that order are taken from one of the most significant poems in *Orillas*, "Saint Escolastica" ("Santa Escolástica" 622–26), culmination and synthesis of her major themes: sorrow of life, struggle with self, search for meaning, hope for salvation, and art as a way to higher consciousness. It describes a moment of revelation in which dream, art, poetry, and God are fused.

The poem, narrated in the first person, begins as the poet wanders through the gray, rain-drenched city of Santiago, "fleeing from my shadow." The city is deserted, frozen in its stodgy inactivity, seeming to belie its days of glory and vitality. As she passes the cathedral, the giant bulk of the towers seems about to fall upon her. The city evokes in her both hate and love; it crushes her dreams and imposes "arid truth" upon her. Despair fills her soul: "And I wished to die!" Her wounded and rebellious spirit questions defiantly: "Why, since there is a God, does Hell triumph?" (*"¿por qué, ya que hay Dios, vence el infierno?"* 624).

She enters the temple (in the convent of San Martín Pinario) seeking consolation and inspiration in the sensuous-mystical atmosphere of silence and fragrance. Her eyes search the altar for some heavenly ray of light. At that moment, the sun breaks through the clouds and penetrates the windows. It strikes the statue of Saint Escolastica and the angel, who are portrayed in a moment of ecstasy.[8] Transfixed, the poet experiences a mystic-like trance, which she expresses in language much like that of the mystics: "that group . . . wounded me silently . . ." (*"aquel grupo . . . me hirió calladamente . . ."* 626). Her soul is flooded with a radiance of understanding in which beauty, dream, art, poetry, and God become one:

All there was in me of passion and tenderness,
of enthusiasm and fervent and glorious aspirations,
before the wondrous dream realized by the artist,
stirring with life again, resuscitated in my breast.

I felt again the fire which illuminates and creates,
the secret longings, the nameless loves
which like the wind on the aeolian harp, awaken
in the soul its most vibrant notes, its sweetest songs.

And invoking and blessing Him who is altogether beauty,
I bent my knee and bowed my head
before Him, and, deeply moved, I suddenly exclaimed:
"There is art! There is poetry! . . . There must be a Heaven,
for there is God!"

(*Todo cuanto en mí había de pasión y ternura,*
de entusiasmo y fervientes y gloriosos empeños,
ante el sueño admirable que realizó el artista,
volviendo a tomar vida, resucitó en mi pecho.

Sentí otra vez el fuego que ilumina y que crea,
los secretos anhelos, los amores sin nombre,
que como al arpa eólica el viento, al alma arrancan
sus notas más vibrantes, sus más dulces canciones.

Y orando y bendiciendo al que es todo hermosura,
se dobló mi rodilla, mi frente se inclinó
ante Él, y, conturbada, exclamé de repente:
"¡Hay arte! ¡Hay poesía! . . . Debe haber cielo:
hay Dios!" 626)

This is the most joyous cry in all of Rosalía's work, a triumphant insight into the human relationship to the divine through creativity, the dream made real.

This poem may be compared to a similar poem in *New Leaves*, "In the Cathedral" ("*N' a Catredal,*" 426–28), to serve as illustration of the progression toward psychic wholeness evidenced in *The Sar*. In the earlier poem the setting is also a temple (the Cathedral of Santiago de Compostela) and the point of view is the same. The poet marvels at the sculptured images of the saints, but the grotesque figments of medieval imagination—demons and souls in torment—which are carved on the friezes and columns seem to come alive and grimace at her. The sun breaks through the windows in sparkling, varicolored light, and her mind leaps to fantasy; but soon the shadows come again and darkness and mystery prevail, symbolic of her state of soul. She says a prayer to the Virgin of Solitude, and flees, afraid. The mood of fear and torment and the failure to find consolation or liberation, characteristic of *Follas*, contrast dramatically with the spiritual renewal expressed in *Orillas*.

Rosalía's life, cut short at what one might expect to be its midpoint, was full of lived experience and rich in human and self understanding. It culminated artistically in an affirmation of all that is essentially human: thought, speech, dream, pursuit of beauty, art, and love. Sorrow derives from all these, from the sense of their brevity and imperfections and from the realization that, in spite of all that man is capable of conceiving, doing, and knowing, he cannot penetrate with either thought or experience the final mystery. This is the "tragic sense," humanity in man. The poet has travelled the tortured labyrinth of disillusionment and despair. In *En las orillas del Sar*, the ways lead on toward light, unity, and peace.

CHAPTER 8

Prose

I *Prose in Spain in the Nineteenth Century*

DURING the first half of the nineteenth century, roughly the period of Romanticism (1830–1850), the novel was not a strong genre in Spanish literature. There were novels written, of course, but the contributions in poetry and drama have proved more enduring. The novels are rarely reprinted. read, or studied. The first two Romantic novels by Spaniards were written in exile: Trueba y Cossío's *The Black Prince* (1829), published in English in London; and Romón López Soler's *Los bandos de Castilla (The Warring Factions of Castile* [1830]). Between 1831 and 1834, political conditions permitted the return of the liberal emigrés to Spain. Mariano José de Larra, more noted for his *costumbrismo* (local color) and satirical articles, published *El doncel de don Enrique el doliente (The Page of King Henry "the Sick")* in 1834, a novel set in the times of Enrique III, "the Sick" of Castile, 1379–1406. Generally considered of most interest and literary worth among the historical novels is Enrique Gil y Carrasco's *El señor de Bembibre (The Lord of Bembibre* [1844]), which deals with the suppression of the Order of Knights Templar in the fourteenth century. A great deal of fiction was published *por entregas*, in feuilleton or installments. Although some significant works were first printed in this form, it was for the most part the outlet for sentimental thrillers or heart warmers, the soap operas of the day.

José F. Montesinos has remarked, with reference to the hiatus between the great Spanish novels of the seventeenth century and the revival of prose fiction toward the end of the nineteenth century, that "the Spanish novel no longer existed, and did not yet exist."[1] A number of factors contributed to the absence of a truly

100

Spanish novel during this period. An abundance of foreign novels was translated to satisfy the reading public. France, England, and Germany had already gone through Romanticism, and the Spaniards greatly admired such authors as Sir Walter Scott, Goethe, E. T. A. Hoffmann, Bernardin de Saint-Pierre, Chateaubriand, Victor Hugo, George Sand, and the narrative poems of Lord Byron. The novels produced in Spain show strong foreign influence, especially from the historical novels of Sir Walter Scott. Although they substitute Spanish castles for English ones, there is little that is original about them. Social, and at times official, attitudes toward the novel were reprehensive. They were thought to be a bad influence on morals and, at best, a waste of time. The purists objected to translations, thinking that they corrupted the language and introduced pernicious foreign trends.

The most vigorous prose genre during Romanticism was the short, descriptive *costumbrista* article which treated local and colorful subjects from everyday contemporary life. To the city bred, it was a kind of exoticism, and also an expression of nationalistic sentiment. In addition to sharp observation and graphic description, the *costumbrista* pieces could contain humor, criticism, and bitter satire. The recognized masters of the genre are Mariano José de Larra, Serafín Estébañez Calderón, and Ramón de Mesonero Romanos.

An exhaustive study of Spain's Romantic novel remains to be done, though perhaps it merits the oblivion to which it is generally assigned. As Ángel del Río states: "It is cultivated by all the writers, but, for some inexplicable cause in a country with the novelistic tradition of Spain, the genre does not solidify and is today the most definitively forgotten genre of all the Romantic production."[2] If such a study were done, Rosalía and Manuel Murguía might merit a chapter, or at least a mention.

Around mid-century, a new age of Spanish prose began to dawn. The Realistic novel was, in part, an outgrowth of the close observation and interest in things Spanish of *costumbrismo,* of a revived appreciation of Cervantes and the picaresque novels, and of the influence of foreign Realists such as Honoré de Balzac, Gustave Flaubert, Stendhal, William Thackery, and Charles Dickens.

As society became increasingly middle class, the novel became its most characteristic literary genre, reflecting a scientific and pragmatic outlook, an interest in urban as well as rural environments, and a preoccupation with contemporary problems. Members of the prosperous bourgeoisie produced, read, bought, and sold the books, and they liked to study and to read about themselves, their behavior, and their interaction in society. Man's fate no longer lay in the stars, but in biological causality, through the effects of heredity and environment. In the Spanish interpretations of Realism and Naturalism, however, these factors were not absolutely deterministic, their effects being modified by psychological forces and *albedrío* or Christian free will. It was not an age of escape, but of disillusionment, which established a new rapport with Cervantes, Quevedo, and other great *desengañados* (disillusioned ones) of the Baroque. There came to the fore a group of outstanding artists to interpret the Spanish scene and probe the depths of human truths.

Cecilia Bohl de Faber, usually known by her pseudonym, Fernán Caballero, is generally credited as initiator of the Spanish Realistic novel with the publication of *La gaviota* (*The Seagull*) in 1849. Her statement, "the novel is not invented; it is observed," is indicative of the change of emphasis from subjective and imaginative to objective and plausible. The rest of the century was dominated by giants of prose: Pedro Antonio de Alarcón, Juan Valera, José María de Pereda, Emilia Pardo Bazán, Leopoldo Alas [Clarín], Armando Palacio Valdés, Benito Pérez Galdós, and Vincent Blasco Ibáñez.

Rosalía was contemporary with all of these: some forty years younger than Fernán Caballero, but outliving her by only seven years; fourteen years older than her ambitious and aggressive fellow countrywoman (i.e. Galician), Countess Pardo Bazán; and four years older than Galdós. Her prose career, 1859 to 1881, falls between the transition to Realism with prolongation of Romantic tendencies and the unquestionable triumph of Realism around 1870. She knew and read the works of at least those who were actively publishing before the 1880s. In her own day, as in successive decades, her prose escaped general attention. Fernán Caballero and Emilia Pardo Bazán took somewhat belated notice of her. It was an age dominated by major novelists and the lesser voices were lost in the wilderness.

Prose occupies a considerable portion of Rosalía's literary production: four novels, short stories of varying lengths, articles, and prologues. Her second published work was a novel, and she published one three years before her death. She cultivated prose seriously and found publishers; some of her works have had several editions. After her early residence in Madrid, she did not participate actively in literary circles nor compete for attention. Ill health, domestic and maternal concerns, and her own predilection for tranquility and retirement in Galicia took precedence over the pursuit of literary renown. Her success as a regional writer, the acceptance of her poetry, and the domination of the literary scene by prolific and superb prose writers relegated her prose to obscurity. It is through interest in her as a poet and person that later scholarship has examined this aspect of her work.

II   La hija del mar (Child from the Sea)

Rosalía's first novel, *La hija del mar (Child from the Sea)*, 1859, was dedicated to her husband, Manuel Murguía. It is offered as "a fond remembrance of happy days . . ." (*"cariñoso recuerdo de algunos días de felicidad . . ."* 660), a literary gesture her novelist husband would appreciate (Murguía also brought out two novels that same year). In the brief prologue, the author apologizes for her daring as a woman in publishing a book. She cites in her defense the French author Malebranche and the Galician scholar Benito Jerónimo Feijoo, proponents of woman's intellectual emancipation, and goes on to list a number of illustrious women, such as Mme de Staël, George Sand, Saint Teresa, and Sappho. She does not argue with the idea that women serve only for domestic duties and that those who enter public life are "execrable." Still, in her day and age it was beginning to be admitted that women had souls and could think, and might indulge in the belief that they could write books: ". . . today, new Lazaruses, we have gathered these crumbs of liberty from the table of the rich man, who is called the nineteenth century." (662).

Once her verses were in print (*La flor*, 1857), the publication of the novel was inevitable, for "once the first step is taken on the path of perdition, the rest follow after." (662). She has no pretensions or illusions: ". . . one more book in the sea of current publications is like a drop of water in the Ocean." (662). She begs patience of her readers and hopes that they will soon forget the book and that it was written by a woman, "for it is still not permitted to women to write what they feel and what they know." (662). This is the girl of twenty-two, who was to spend the rest of her life writing what she felt and what she knew. *La hija del mar (Child from the Sea)* is a lengthy and rambling novel of twenty chapters, which are given titles such as "Emotions," "Torments," "The Madwoman," "Surprise," "Crisis," and the like. Each chapter bears an epigraph, giving an indication of Rosalía's literary enthusiasms at that time. These include Ossian, George Sand, Byron, San Juan, Goethe, Góngora, José Zorrilla, and Bernardin de Saint-Pierre, among many others.

The story is set in the fishing village of Mugía, site of the shrine of Our Lady of the Ship, on the peninsula of Finisterre.[3] The action begins with an animated scene of fishermen pulling in the catch, struggling against a stormy sea. In the village lives Teresa, the heroine of the novel, a girl of dark beauty whose refinement, melancholy, and mysterious air set her apart from the simple fisherfolk. The reader learns that she is illegitimate and was abandoned by her mother. After a brief marriage, she was in turn abandoned by her husband and lives alone with her baby son.

As the men land the catch, the hearty fisherman, Lorenzo, appears with a mysterious bundle—a tiny baby girl he has found on the promontory Black Rock. It is decided to give the baby to Teresa. At that moment, her own child is swept into the stormy sea. Teresa gives her "child from the sea" the name Esperanza (Hope), and the baby grows into a lovely young girl with golden hair and dark eyes. An idyllic and ill fated love develops between Esperanza and Fausto, son of the fisherman Lorenzo.

Teresa's husband returns in the guise of the pirate Alberto. He takes her on board his luxurious ship and is very ardent. Esperanza is captured and brought on board also. Alberto soon turns his attentions to Esperanza and holds both women prisoners in his country palace. Teresa struggles to protect her daughter and manages to escape in search of help. Fausto has attempted to kill Alberto and rescue Esperanza. Consumed by passion, grief, and hatred of his rival, the youth succumbs to a fever. As he is dying, he confesses to his father that he has tried to kill a man. Lorenzo searches for his son's intended victim to ask his pardon so that Fausto will not die in mortal sin. He arrives at Alberto's palace while the servants are pursuing Teresa and confronts the angry Alberto. In the confusion, Esperanza escapes.

In her flight, Esperanza passes Fausto's hut. He sees her and pursues her, but she does not recognize him. The death knell is tolling for Fausto, and a candlelight procession—priests coming to administer last rites to Fausto—approaches. Esperanza thinks it is a ghostly procession led by the shadowy figure of Fausto. Esperanza and Fausto fall exhausted on the sand. When Esperanza awakens, she discovers Fausto is dead and runs to his home to tell Lorenzo. The priests will not administer extreme unction to Fausto and he is denied Christian burial. The folk bury him secretly in the sea. Esperanza witnesses the eerie scene from the shadows and cries out, frightening the superstitious villagers. She goes mad. Flames and smoke are seen in the distance, where Teresa has set fire to Alberto's palace.

But this is not the end of the story. The scene shifts to an unnamed place where a beautiful insane girl is under the care of a man called Ansot and the Dr. Ricarder. Ansot loves the girl and for the first time in his depraved life, he is stirred by noble motives—to save the girl and win her love. He recalls his past and his wife, Candora, whom he abandoned because he thought her unfaithful and from whom he took the daughter he believed belonged to another man. Candora appears and tries to kill him, but he escapes.

The sick girl, frightened by a swallow (she has a maniacal fear of birds), falls into a pool and is saved from drowning by the housekeeper, Ángela, a virtuous and gentle woman. As the girl hovers between life and death, Ansot reverts to his old violent ways. Warned that he is being pursued by the law, he flees with three companions. The girl, staring at the reflection of a white dove, again falls into the pool. Rescued, she awakens sane, but remembers nothing. The doctor asks Ángela to tell her a sad story, to shock her into consciousness and feeling. As Ángela begins, Candora reappears and talks deliriously to the golden-haired girl who resembles her own lost daughter. She mentions the name of Alberto and the girl's memory begins to come back. Ángela reveals her own and Candora's stories.

Candora, raised in America by a cruel aunt, meets and elopes with the adventurer Alberto. He soon tires of her and abandons her on the shores of Galicia, where she is befriended by a young sailor, Daniel. She bears Alberto's child, but when he returns he accuses her of unfaithfulness with the innocent Daniel. He takes them out to sea with his pirate horde, drowns Daniel and abandons the baby on Black Rock. Ángela, who loved Daniel, has patiently awaited her chance to avenge his death. The mad girl realizes that she is Alberto's daughter, and that Candora is her real mother. Ángela, discovering the identities of Esperanza and Alberto Ansot, swears to avenge the wrongs done to them all.

Teresa reappears, having followed Alberto through many lands.

She warns him that his crimes have been found out and that he has been accused by Ángela. Captured, Alberto Ansot is hanged as pirate, assassin, and incendiary. Ángela witnesses his death, but is led away by Dr. Ricarder. Teresa knows that it is just, although she still loves Alberto. Poetic justice is meted out, but it makes no one happy. Teresa still seeks her lost daughter, and Esperanza wanders in search of her adoptive mother. In despair, Esperanza jumps into the sea. Her body is washed up near Teresa, who kisses her dead daughter for the last time as the sea again claims its child.

The plot is indeed complicated and disjointed, yet it can be reduced to some sort of coherency. It consists of a double ring of seduction and abandonment perpetrated by the fascinating and malevolent Alberto. The first cycle involves Candora ("Innocence"), the next, Teresa. The rings are connected by Esperanza ("Hope"), who is the child of Alberto and Candora, abducted by her father and abandoned, adopted by Teresa, Alberto's other wife, and again carried off by Alberto. The sea is the fate or destiny which operates in all their lives: it claims the child of Alberto and Teresa, the little boy lost in the storm; Esperanza, the miraculous child of the title, appears from the sea and eventually returns to it; Esperanza's beloved Fausto is buried in the sea; Alberto, the pirate, rides the sea and consigns two people to it—Daniel, whom he drowns, and Fausto, who dies as a consequence of Alberto's abduction of Esperanza. The sea is both love and death, which is not incompatible with its role as fate.

The central and best-delineated character is Teresa, a star-crossed heroine, exceptional and alienated from society. Her destiny is loneliness; she is illegitimate, orphaned, abandoned by her husband, and bereft of her children. Her external appearance reveals her unusual inner qualities; she is described as having a somber beauty, too aristocratic in mein and manner for her rude surroundings. Furthermore, she is a poet, possessed of those higher sensibilities which doom her to restlessness and suffering. Consequently, she is "mad," obsessed and visionary. Her talents are lost because of her isolation; her mind and behavior strange because of her imagination and dreaminess.

Rosalía put a great deal of her inner self into this character. She develops at length the independent and poetic temperament of Teresa and the solitude and moral suffering to which she is subjected, which are the mad poet's lot. The name Teresa is that of

Rosalía's mother, and the preoccupation with passionate and unhappy love, abandonment, and illegitimacy may derive from circumstances in her own life. The novel may be said to be spiritually
autobiographical in certain respects.

Esperanza is the fair heroine, mysterious "child of the sea," representing innocence, ideal love, hope. She is the ethereal love object, as either child or beloved, of the other principal characters. As
an impossible ideal, she is never quite earthly, and is separated and
protected from life and the world by insanity (hers is a different sort
of madness from Teresa's) and death. On another level, Esperanza
can be interpreted as a symbol of the soul or unconscious. She arises
and disappears into the sea, and is associated with pools of water,
forests, and birds. She might be seen as the anima or soul-image of
Alberto, moving him to regeneration, and his incestuous desire for
her (although, of course, he does not know her identity) as his
symbolic search for union with the essence of himself.

The three principal male characters tend to be all of a piece,
either very good in the case of Fausto and his father Lorenzo, or
thoroughly wicked in the case of Alberto. Lorenzo represents rugged, paternal simplicity. He has a minor role, but a certain flesh and
blood conviction about him. Fausto represents purity and innocence, and hence cannot survive; he is doomed by the fateful and
impossible love for Esperanza. Alberto occupies center stage a great
deal of the time, particularly in the second part of the book. He is
incredibly villainous, yet the author shows a certain sympathetic
fascination with him. His seductive dash is convincing, and under
the alias of Ansot he undergoes some moral introspection and almost
reforms. He is in some ways the diabolic Romantic hero.

The portrayal of the masculine characters leads to speculation on
the young Rosalía's view of men. The extent of her acquaintance
with her father is not known, and throughout her work the preoccupation with the father figure is not a major theme, although some
critics have detected what they believe to be indirect allusions.[4]
Her mother's experience and others like it from the village and from
literature influenced her attitude toward passionate love and its
consequences, which are seen as inevitable, forgiveable, and disas-
trous. In *La hija del mar* men appear as both good and bad. It is
certainly not a one sided view.

The style of the novel is diffuse and immature. The author assumes the omniscient point of view, revealing to the reader the

characters' appearance and actions, as well as their inner thoughts and feelings. She occasionally inserts personal comments expressing her views on the evils of superstition (in connection with the burial of Fausto), the inequities of society (the hovels of peasants in contrast to Alberto's palace), and men's oppression of women.

Nature is portrayed with the mystical awe of the Romantic and complements the characters' moods. The setting, at least in the first part, is a real place—the coastline of Galicia near Finisterre, a suitably violent, majestic, and lonely spot. Rosalía's loving intimacy with nature lends particular vividness to her descriptions of storms, tossing seas, lush forests, and desolate windswept shores. Descriptions of nature are frequently offered as redeeming aspects of Romantic novels. Rosalía, in her prose as well as her poetry, excells in the depiction of nature, painting masterful vistas of color, movement, sound, and mood.

Child from the Sea is a novel difficult to classify, either as to movement or genre. It has many obvious elements of Romanticism: sustained emotional intensity, improbable situations and events, focus on the exceptional in character, extremes of good and evil, fantasy and lore. Its author was, after all, twenty-two years old and steeped in the Romanticism of her formative years, as the epigraphs bear witness. It is not a historical novel; the setting is contemporary and part of the action takes place in a specific part of Galicia. It is, rather, a novel of adventure and sentiment, set somewhere outside time and place. The ways of the folk and the effects of love and tragedy are timeless, and much of the action unfolds in a realm of fantasy. There are touches of *costumbrismo*—descriptions of the life and activities of the fishermen, allusion to folk practices and beliefs, and incorporation of colloquial expressions in the characters' speech. For the most part the diction is refined and even stilted and the Galician touches are vivid, but incidental rather than integral to the story. In the second part, the author is off into contrived settings such as pirate ships and luxurious palaces which appear out of nowhere, and the landscapes are dreamlike. The subjective-lyrical quality is dominant and the book is replete with symbolic elements, which Rosalía may or may not have intended or consciously worked out. In view of her tendency to project psychic contents into her works, as evidenced in the poetry, a careful analysis of the symbolism would be valid and therein might lie a thread of unity and a key to meaning of this confused and puzzling novel.

Themes which are to become characteristic of Rosalía's work appear in the novel. The story and the characters (Teresa in particular) are sorrowful, and the word *dolor* occurs frequently; there is preoccupation with solitude, madness, and the poetic temperament. The image of the *sombra* also appears—the vision of her lost child Esperanza which leads Teresa in her desperate search (830). In spite of its many defects as a novel, *Child from the Sea* represents a considerable achievement for its youthful author. It shows skill and inventiveness in spinning out a narrative, a certain psychological profundity in its characters and themes, and great sensitivity and verbal command in lyrical and descriptive passages. It is of most interest for the insight it offers, along with the first book of poetry, *La flor* (1857), into the early literary development of the author.

III Flavio

Rosalía's second novel, *Flavio* (the name of the principal character), was published in 1861. It bears the modest subtitle "attempt at a novel" ("*ensayo de una novela*"). There is no preface. The plot deals with the turbulent love of two strong willed protagonists, Flavio and Mara, and hinges on conflict of characters rather than on events or outside forces. The love of Flavio and Mara is the proverbial irresistible force which meets the immovable object. Flavio is the wild, proud "natural man" (although he possesses an almost decadent refinement as well), raised in isolation as heir to the remote and noble estate of the Brediván family. Set free by the death of his parents, he leaves his somber "prison" and sets out to explore the world in quest of liberty. He is almost totally ignorant of life, selfish and egotistical in an infantile way.

As he flees from his home, he passes through a lyrical nocturnal landscape and stops to investigate a fantastic scene of lights and dancing in the forest. He has happened onto an elegant outdoor ball. Unschooled in the ways of polite society, he glowers and lurks like a fawn. He sees beautiful women for the first time, and is overwhelmed. They are not pretty and weak creatures at all, as he was previously told, but aery and sublime as they move gracefully through the sylvan forest in diaphanous gowns. The girls notice him and tease him; he is humiliated by their flirtatiousness and reacts with belligerence. His brusque manners, which mask wounded pride, cause the girls to mock him, angering him further. He meets a girl (Mara) of unconventional beauty and serious manner who does not flirt nor appear perturbed by his clumsiness and hostility. She is fascinated with him, as he is so different from the courtly, artificial gentlemen. She somewhat fears his rather mad behavior and her own pride will not suffer his overwhelming ego. His emotions are as quick as his temper, however, and they soon realize that they are two sensitive, passionate, and unique souls irresistibly drawn to each other. There begins the strange love duel which occupies the book.

Mara is Flavio's ideal woman, his spiritual beloved, but he is up against her own pride, will, and ideals. She is educated and refined, and belongs to a totally alien world of cultured society. For Mara, Flavio represents a love to which she can dedicate her heart and soul, a man of strong independence, sincerity, and idealism like her own, but he is impulsive, anti-social and possessive. He cannot subject himself to social formalities and is insanely jealous of her friends and social obligations, especially of an old friend and suitor, Ricardo, his bitter rival. Flavio follows Mara to the city, but is not at ease there. He feels betrayed by her behavior, unable to understand her reserve in public and the ridicule of her friends at his violent outbursts. She is torn between devotion and loyalty to him and a way of life she cannot leave.

This basic plot is complicated by a subplot which might be taken as extraneous, but for its additional revelation of Flavio's character and its function in precipitating the outcome. Flavio is attracted, in a fraternal way, to the lovely girl Rosa, daughter of the mistress of the house where he lodges. The girl is left an orphan on the death of her mother and as she is about to be evicted from her home, it is fortuitously discovered that Flavio is the heir and rightful owner. He gives the property to Rosa and her aunt, although they protest that the girl's reputation may be questioned. Her mother had had to compromise her honor in order to live and raise her daughter there. Flavio doesn't understand all that about honor (which Mara has tried to explain to him before) and swears to be Rosa's protector. The girl loves him, but he feels only fondness for her. Flavio, disillusioned and desperate, meditates on life and death and attempts suicide by drowning. He is saved by a solitary young man, the doctor Luis, who becomes his friend.

Mara hears gossip about Rosa and Flavio and confronts the innocent and uncomprehending Flavio. They quarrel, then there is a reconciliation. Mara devotes herself to Flavio like a slave, but is fearful of his moods. The story concludes in an atmosphere of Carnaval—fantasy, delirium, and excess. Flavio forbids Mara to go to the masked ball, and she obeys to prove her faithfulness. At the ball, Flavio is seduced by two masked women and loses his inno-cence. He becomes cynical, deceives and abandons Rosa and their child, and marries a rich old woman whose wealth he soon inherits. He lives in sybaritic splendor, joking about his past. Mara, hearing indirectly of Flavio's behavior, retires to the country with her mother.

Flavio is the romantic hero—sullen, handsome, daring, rebel-lious, noble, sensitive, and melancholic. He embodies the dilemma of the Romantic temperament whose ideals of absolute freedom and perfection come to a deadlock with the necessity of maturing and assuming the responsibilities of living within society. The usual so-lutions for the Romantic hero are death or insanity, thus avoiding compromise with reality. Flavio's reaction, although he narrowly escapes the other two, is a third possibility—decadence.

Mara is one of Rosalía's strongest characters. She is proud and independent of spirit and quietly unconventional. She refuses the humiliation of a marriage of convenience and a life of social inanities, wherein a woman may enjoy a hollow status while serving as an accessory to male vanity. Her aspirations are for intellectual and spiritual as well as emotional fulfullment. Also, Mara is a poet, but writes in secret, for this is not deemed a fitting activity for a woman: ". . . A woman who dares to transfer to paper her most hidden sentiments, those sentiments which no one should penetrate . . . , those at which she herself should blush, perhaps . . . Madness! . . ." (911). Yet she is driven by her restless imagination, inner pas-sions, and the caprices of inspiration. After all, she ponders, the characteristics usually attributed to women—moodiness, nervous sensibility, propensity for melancholy, and an innate desire for that which is unobtainable—should fit them admirably for being poets. ". . . Men can't even say that they are hysterical, and that is such a fecund muse! . . ." (912). Through Mara, Rosalía enunciates the theme of the talented woman who aspires to creativity in spite of the reprehension of society.

Mara's character defects (or virtues, perhaps) are vanity and pride (i.e., self-esteem and sense of honor). Her dream of enjoying perfect love while maintaining her independence and integrity cannot be realized. Communication with the beloved is impossible. Sadder, if wiser, she is left with the solitary struggle of inner desires versus outward composure. Both Flavio and Mara must remain solitary. Mara becomes, not a decadent, but a realist.

The style of this second novel is smoother and more sophisticated. It is narrated in third person, with many monologues and dialogues. The author does not intervene overtly, but gives vent to her ideas and feelings through the characters. The structure is a pulsation of emotions, a disquisition on temperament, love, and will. The settings are never specific. Nature as a background is luxuriant and idyllic or somber and stormy to complement the mood of the scene. The city with its stultifying restrictions and hypocritical public behavior serves as a contrast to the naturalness and freedom of the country. Place names are vague, but the locale is somewhere in Galicia. The city is Santiago in thin disguise—ancient, rainy, gray, and oppressive with an "old and poetic cathedral." The rare interiors are not vividly described; those associated with Flavio are sumptuous and, as in *Child from the Sea,* the effete luxury is linked to a certain degeneracy.

Flavio, like the first novel, cannot be strictly classified. There are many Romantic elements—the temperaments of the principal characters, indifference to the exigencies of everyday life, fantastic or dreamlike settings. Yet the author takes a knowledgeable point of view toward this very Romanticism, and reveals an awareness of transition, in herself as well as in the times and literary trends. It could best be termed psychological, for its characters offer a complex study of emotions and motives, presented with psychological depth and veracity. Much of the book is devoted to introspective analyses on the part of Flavio and Mara. These two characters are multi-faceted, changeable, and enigmatic, which is to say they are people rather than types or symbols. Society is perhaps the real villain, with its restraints, false values, artificial behavior, concern for propriety, and malicious gossip. In this respect, *Flavio* resembles the Realistic novel.

Rosalía explores some of her favorite themes in this novel: the contrary nature of human love, the inner realities of poets and poetry, individual liberty, aversion to hypocrisy, and the position of women. The novel, in its study of two anguished characters, can be seen to represent the drama of conflicting elements within Rosalía herself—rebellious individualism and soaring idealism in opposition to a rational and analytical comprehension of the world.

IV El caballero de las botas azules
(The Gentleman of the Blue Boots)

El caballero de las botas azules (*The Gentleman of the Blue Boots*), 1867, cannot be said to be well-known, but among Rosalía's novels, it has been the only one to receive much mention. Writers such as Fernán Caballero, and the later Ramón Gómez de la Serna (1891–1963) took favorable notice of it. Murguía discusses this novel in some length in *Los precursores* (*The Precursors*).[5] It is subtitled "Strange Tale" (*"Cuento extraño"*), which puts the reader in the proper mood and warns him not to expect *costumbrismo* or realism, even if he had, considering the title. The novel is prefaced by a dialogue, "A Man and a Muse" (*"Un hombre y una musa"*), which is one of Rosalía's most interesting critical statements. It might be considered a work in its own right, but is thematically related to *El caballero,* so a presentation of it belongs here.

In an unusual variation on an old theme, the poet summons his muse, who turns out not to be the sweet, feminine ideal he is expecting. From behind the dark cloud which hides her, the muse berates the aspirant writer for his enslavement to tradition and trite subjects. She is critical, contentious, and insulting. Finally she reveals herself, and emerges from the cloud of mist—a grotesque figure in strange attire: tall and stately, dressed in a tunic, boots, and widebrimmed hat. The writer is appalled and calls her monstrous and evil. He asks her name and she replies *"Novedad"* (*"The New"*); her message is: "Shake off silly scruples and break once and for all with preoccupations of the past." (*"Déjate de vanos escrúpulos y rompe de una vez con las pasadas preocupaciones."* 1176). This statement anticipates the declarations of Rubén Darío and other Modernists. The writer finally comprehends and sets out "with new and satirical spirit" to look ironically and penetratingly at his age. As she departs, the Muse tells him: "What greater ambition can a man have in this century of caricatures than to create his own and that of others before an appreciative audience?" (*"¿Qué más puede ambicionar un hombre en el siglo de las caricaturas que hacer la suya propia y la de los demás ante un auditorio conmovido?"* 1176). In the spirit of the Muse's words, the novel *El caballero de las botas azules* (*The Gentleman of the Blue Boots*) sets out to caricature its age and protest the bad literature currently in vogue.

The title of the novel refers to the principal character. This gentleman is described as youthful and elegant, with abundant black hair, a marble-white face, and an ironic expression. He is dressed in black, with gleaming blue knee boots. His necktie is a white eagle with spread wings and he carries a diamond-studded ebony stick with a bell on the end. This astounding and mysterious creature arrives in Madrid and sets the whole town on its ear, affecting all levels of society. When not identified by his blue boots, he is known as the Duke of Glory *(el Duque de la Gloria)*. He has come with two missions: to publish the Book of Books *(Libro de los libros)* containing the secrets of the Sage of Moravia, and to "bell the cat" (a reference to the fable of the mice who devise a plan to put a bell on the cat who is causing devastation among them, but the plan does not include how to attach the bell to the cat or who is going to do it). He begins by disturbing the peace and quiet of the wealthy and eccentric Señor de la Albuérniga, whose response to the insanity and confusion of the world is to withdraw into his velvet-lined isolation and read philosophy. The garish duke is a very resented intruder, but a wary sort of friendship develops between them.

The duke has society at his feet. He is noble, compelling, clever, and mysterious. And those marvelous boots! And that exotic necktie! He is courted, imitated, hated, and loved. All of the ladies of high society are intrigued with him and seek his favor. They are lovely, elegant, intelligent, but live frivolous and futile lives. He accepts their invitations, enjoys making them wait or catching them in *déshabillé*, and humbles them all. At a ball in his honor, the duke does not appear until the guests have drunk, danced, and bored themselves to exhaustion. The duke irritates editors, writers, and critics with his devastating remarks about the current level of literary and journalistic production. He publishes his own newspaper, *Las Tinieblas* (darkness), and forbids the other papers to talk about him. The ladies, influenced by the glamorous duke, become critical of fashionable literature. Both the men and the women are ridiculous.

The women are rebelling against their subjugation, but in a frivolous, ineffectual manner. They cannot forego their idle pastimes and extravagant clothes. The duke asks a countess if the women do spinning, knitting, or sewing. Horrors! Those are plebeian tasks. He tells her of his great-grandmother, a countess and a virtuous, industrious woman who spun, surrounded by her attendants. He confesses that he is seeking that kind of woman.

Spinning becomes fashionable among the society ladies, who organize a spinning group and affect rough and simple attire—but wear diamond tiaras in their hair. The middle class comes in for its share of criticism. The reader is introduced to the families of a doctor, a lawyer, a civil servant, and a military officer, who vie for status among themselves. The husbands are harrassed by the extravagances of their wives and daughters, who insist on living like the upper class and have to hock heirlooms for the latest fad. The style this particular year demands eagles on hats, blue boots, and bells on flounces. The duke suggests that the women knit to earn money for their expenses and dowries, and is met with another horrified reaction: "Are we to toil for money as though we were miserable working-women!" (*"¡Trabajar por dinero, como si fuésemos miserables obreras!"* 1337).

A subplot provides some human interest. Doña Dorotea, a prim and modest school mistress, and her niece, Mariquita, live with honest decency in an humble section of town. Mariquita is engaged to the youth Melchor, but she meets and falls in love with the duke, rejecting the timid and awkward boy. Her father and aunt are dismayed at her resistance to Melchor, and also alarmed because the neighborhood has seen the duke take Mariquita's hand in public. Her reputation is threatened, and she is a disobedient daughter. (These incidents allow Rosalía to comment on arranged marriages and prudish morality.) The duke convinces the girl that he is old and she would not be happy. He patches things up with Melchor and the family. It is finally revealed that the duke had been in love with Dorotea long ago.

As the story comes to its close, a mysterious blind man appears in town (another guise of the duke), singing satirical ditties and speaking of the prophet Moravo. The Book of Books will soon appear, and the cat will soon be belled. The public is curious and skeptical. The duke gives a grand feast in the palace of Albuérniga, in an atmosphere of mystery. A fountain is unveiled which spouts books which fall into the deep "pit of modern knowledge." The society ladies appear dressed as slaves. The duke shocks the company by presenting the modest Doña Dorotea as his beloved, still beautiful in his eyes. He then says farewell and the lights go out. The guests panic and search for exists. They feel something around their throats and hear loud ringing of bells. When they finally reach the street, they discover that each person is wearing a bell around his neck. The next day the angry public storms the palace, but the duke is not there. They are met by a shower of tiny books bound in velvet with gold clasps—the Book of Books. Inside the palace they find a reclining statue of the duke. At his feet is a huge cat with a pen in its mouth and a bell around its neck.

The characters of this book are, for the most part, cardboard cutouts or puppets—intentionally so, and in line with the purport of the book. The unity is provided by the character of the duke, moral and intellectual gadfly, mysterious and multifaceted. In his guise as the Gentleman of the Blue Boots he is arrogant, irreverent, and almost supernatural. In his private moments, he is an aging, disillusioned, and sentimental mortal who wears makeup of marble paste. The author takes several points of view throughout the novel, employing the devices of dialogue and epistle as well as narration. Mostly, however, she is omniscient, pulling the strings of her puppets and inserting observations of her own. She admits that her style is rambling and has to be set back on the track occasionally.

The Gentleman is not a Realistic novel in the strict sense of adhering to the objective portrayal of contemporary problems and manners, but it is definitely attuned to its times. It is specifically set in Madrid in the present, and is a scathing (albeit humorous) criticism of customs, institutions, and attitudes. Barbs are levelled primarily at the middle and upper classes and their false pursuits. Fashion, education, writers, publishers, women, marriage customs, and esthetic tastes are exposed. The one great evil—here as elsewhere in Rosalía's works—is hypocrisy. Fantasy is an effective vehicle for satire (as in *Gulliver's Travels*), allowing the author to discuss real issues while remaining free from the limits of logic and everyday reality in order to manipulate situations and characters at will. The connection with real life is metaphorical.

Literature is her principal target. She speaks of "the pernicious fecundity" of certain poets; "terribly Spanish-historical" novels; and "pages which are flimsily written, but perfectly imprinted." She deplores the sentimental drivel dispensed in serial form under such titles as "The Honorable Woman," "Poverty without Stain," and "Love Sacrificed." She even criticizes herself. During a literary discussion, one of her characters remarks: ". . . I was incensed by my recent reading of an unknown novel which bears the title *The Gentleman of the Blue Boots*. In it, a certain sly humor, as Cervantes would say, pretensions which trail off into infinity, inconceivable audacity, and thought, if indeed it contains any, which no one can figure out, mingle woefully with an absolute lack of talent. I have read half of it and I still don't know in what chapter it begins, since it seems to begin everywhere at once. . . ." (". . . *me ha indignado la reciente lectura de una novela desconocida que lleva por epígrafe* EL CABALLERO DE LAS BOTAS AZULES. *En ella, una gracia bellaca, como diría Cervantes, unas pretensiones que se pierden en lo infinito, una audacia inconcebible y un pensamiento, si es que alguno encierra, que nadie acierta a adivinar, se hermanan lastimosamente con una falta absoluta de ingenio. He leído la mitad y no puedo saber todavía en qué capítulo empieza, puesto que es en todas a la vez. . . ."* 1375).

The Gentleman is a book with a message, so it is permissible to attach meanings to things. Such items as the statue of Modesty, the fountain which spouts books into the "pit of modern knowledge," the cat, and the bells clearly reveal their significance. The culprit (cat) turns out to be Everybody. The accouterments of the duke—blue boots, eagle necktie, stick or wand with bell—are more ambiguous, but the color blue suggests truth and both the color and material of the gentleman's boots cannot be falsified. The eagle perhaps represents liberty, and its whiteness, truth. The bell, connected to the "belling the cat" motif, would imply that truth cannot be hidden. The puzzling figure of the duke, with his white mask, sardonic smile, and elusive identity, cannot be reduced to simple labels. As Murguía concludes in his discussion of the book that, just as the characters are constantly asking each other "What can he be?" "What can he not be?" (*"¿Qué será? ¿Qué no será?"*), the reader has the same questions in mind upon finishing the book.[6] And Rosalía is slyly laughing. In *El caballero de las botas azules*, Rosalía offers a penetrating satire of her times and an ironical treatment of the eternal human comedy, which gives the book a lasting freshness and relevancy. She reveals a sparkling facet of humor in the creation of some superbly funny scenes.

V   El primer loco (The First Madman)

Rosalía's last novel, *El primer loco* (*The First Madman*), 1881, is also subtitled "Strange Tale" (*"Cuento extraño"*), as was *El caballero de las botas azules*. It is indeed a strange story, not extroverted, entertaining, and socially conscious like *El caballero*, but meditative and introspective, a study of poetic temperament and madness. The

story begins as two friends are walking and talking at the old Monastery of Conjo (one of Rosalía's favorite places). Luis, the poet, dwells
in an inner world which "fluctuates between the real and the fantastic, between the absurd and the sublime" (1409). His friend, Pedro,
through whom the reader sees the events of the action and behavior
of Luis, is "of clear intelligence and also of tastes and preferences
half romantic, half realistic" (1409). These two personalities, which
complement and counterbalance each other, offer a multiple
perspective on reality.

Luis is recounting his tragic love for Berenice, who, to him, represents the ideal of beauty. Pedro knows the girl too, and considers
her vain and hollow. Berenice at first seems to accept Luis's adoration and the role of fair lady, but she soon becomes bored with him,
and his incomprehensible behavior alarms her. She marries an
American (depicted as gigantic, with florid complexion, crude manners, and jumbled Spanish) whom her father has picked out for her.
Luis refuses to believe that she did this willfully and continues to
adore her and suffer terrible jealousy. A friend of Berenice's who has
been their intercessor and confidante reveals Berenice's side of the
story to Luis. The girl has very ordinary tastes and ambitions, and
has tired of playing the fairy princess. Luis is distasteful and odious
to her.

Luis meets a gypsy, who reads his fortune and tells him to forget
Bernice. His love has become a destructive passion and will have a
bad outcome. Berenice has been elevated by Luis to a deity and a
religion, as in medieval courtly love. Luis returns to Conjo to find a
gathering of peasants who think they are bewitched, being exorcised
by a country priest. He joins them, although he has no faith in the
ceremony. The priest urges him to return later for nine days of
conjuration. Luis wanders in the forest and pursues a vision of Berenice until he falls unconscious. He awakens in the lap of a young
girl, Esmeralda. Mistreated by her stepmother and father, Esmeralda is protected by a country priest who allows her to herd his
goats. She falls madly in love with Luis. Bored by her, he resents
her resemblance to Berenice and transfers his hurt and jealousy to
her. Luis is called to the deathbed of his uncle and guardian, an
aged priest. The uncle exhorts him to desist from his idolatry of
Berenice, and his dying request is that Luis renounce her. He
cannot grant this request, but is deeply moved by the old man's
counsel and decides to reform. First he must release Esmeralda

from a hopeless relationship and provide for her with some of his inheritance. He realizes that Esmeralda is his victim as he is Berenice's. He sees an apparition of Esmeralda on his doorstep and when he returns to Conjo to search for her, he finds that she has died of love and rejection. Luis plans to found an insane asylum for unfortunates, with whom he sympathizes and identifies.

The denouement comes rapidly. As Luis and Pedro walk through the forest, a hawk kills a magpie at their feet, which they interpret as an omen. Berenice is also walking in the forest. Luis rushes to her and embraces her, although she resists. Luis and her husband struggle, but Pedro and a servant intervene. Luis has gone raving mad. Berenice is injured and frightened. When her child is born, it is dead. Luis dies insane, calling for Berenice. He is cared for by Pedro in the abandoned monastery which was to become the asylum. Luis is the "first madman" to inhabit it.

El primer loco bears a strong resemblance in themes and characters to the earlier novels. Luis is reminiscent of Flavio as a study of the Romantic temperament which cannot come to terms with logical reality. He is more visionary and philosophical, and the book is devoted to his search for reality beyond reason. None of the women characters have the individuality of Mara in *Flavio*. Berenice is seen only through the eyes of others; the reader never directly knows her.

The author assumes the third person point of view in this novel and remains totally apart from the action. There is extensive use of dialogue, and a large part of the text is first person narrative by Luis, which at times approaches a stream of consciousness technique. Coming chronologically as it does after *El caballero de las botas azules*, so different in character, it might seem to be a regression to an earlier period, but its controlled style would indicate that it is a later and more mature work. The time, although taken to be contemporary, is vague and irrelevant; the settings are sylvan and pastoral. *El primer loco* takes place in that favorite realm of Rosalía, where illusion and reality, sanity and madness, blend and are confused. Reality fluctuates according to the various perspectives of the characters. Ultimately, it lies in the mind. Berenice the ideal is more real than the mortal form which inspired her. There is a strong presence of the supernatural, or super-rational, throughout the book—superstitions, apparitions, insanity itself. Luis (Rosalía) sees in the lore of the folk an expression of the higher truths of feeling and spirit; he tells Pedro: "One day read some of the beautiful traditions of our country . . . do not look to science or cold reason . . . but only to sentiment, which is the only thing which has the power to connect us with that which cannot be measured nor touched and is invisible to mortal eyes. . . ." ("*Lee un día alguna de las hermosas tradiciones de nuestro país . . . no apelando a la ciencia ni a la fría razón . . . sino únicamente al sentimiento, que es el único que tiene el poder de communicarnos con lo que ni se mide ni se palpa y es invisible a los mortales ojos. . . .*" 1485).

At the end, Pedro and the reader are left pondering this mysterious, poetic "strange tale."

VI *Short Prose Fiction*

A. "*Conto gallego. Os dous amigos e a viuda*"
   ("Galician Tale. The Two Friends and the Widow")

This short story is Rosalía's only prose work in Galician. She remarked in a footnote to the long narrative poem in *Cantares*, "Vidal" (XXV, 332–43), that since she had no plan to compile a collection of regional stories, she had versified the tale of Vidal for inclusion in the volume of poetry. However, she may have at one time considered such a collection, for the manuscript of "Galician Tale" is headed with the numeral I. The story was probably composed sometime after 1863, but was not published until 1923.[7]

The lighthearted yarn was probably inspired by a folk tale and is full of country witticisms and customs. The subtitle—"Two Friends and the Widow"—gives some clue to the content. Two old friends, Lourenzo and Xan, have differing views on women and marriage. Xan defends them; Lourenzo is the skeptic, preferring his freedom and mistrusting the fair sex. He repeats the aphorisms: "women are devils," and "they're all made of the same stuff and limp on the same foot." To prove to Xan how fickle women are, Lourenzo bets his friend that he can get a certain widow to promise to marry him that same night and to set the wedding for a month later. It's a bet, and Xan puts up his mule.

The funeral of the widow's late husband is in progress and Lourenzo joins the procession, pretending to be nephew and heir of the deceased. He explains to the woman that she has never met him because he comes from another town. As solicitous "next of kin" he accompanies the bereaved woman home. She gives him supper and a room for the night. Xan hides in the stable downstairs, anxiously eavesdropping. During the night, the widow feels cold and Lourenzo gallantly offers to share his bed. She hesitates, but weakens as Lourenzo cajoles her. Xan, overhearing, is desperate at the thought of losing the bet (and his mule). He yells, "the house is burning!" Lourenzo responds, "it isn't the house, it's just the embers," and hastily takes off after Xan, telling the widow to wait, for he'll be back. That was a hundred years ago, and he hasn't come back yet. "Galician Tale" is a charming example of Rosalía's sprightly narrative style, sympathy for the folk, and appreciation of humor.

B. *Ruinas. Desdichas de tres vidas ejemplares*
   (Ruins. Misfortunes of Three Exemplary Lives)

This narrative might be classified as a long short story or a novelette. It first appeared in the periodical *El Museo Universal* in Madrid in 1866. *Ruinas* is a study of three "living ruins," social misfits who are survivors of other times, isolated and strange amidst contemporary village folk. The three include a woman and two men. Doña Isabel Salgado y Peñaranda and her cat Florindo live on a small pension from a dwindling inheritance. Of genteel breeding and aristocratic ancestry, Doña Isabel hasn't bothered to change with the times, and proudly wears her threadbare finery from bygone days when she was belle of the town. She is a favorite at parties, for she writes clever poetry and sings satirical songs. Don Braulio is an elderly merchant ruined by his own generosity who lives on the support of a former employee. Happy and philosophical, he is ridiculed by the town which once enjoyed his largesse. Montenegro is a young man, son of an illustrious family, whose rightful wealth has been usurped by unscrupulous relatives. He and his mother live in poverty while he studies law in order to regain his property. He is tall and gaunt with hair and clothes like someone out of the seventeenth century. Montenegro courts the girls, but they find him unfashionable and ridiculous. His long-suffering mother struggles to keep him afloat while he dreams of what he'll buy her when he recovers his money. He cannot take a job beneath his station—and all jobs are beneath his station.

The three "relics" become friends, drawn together by their mutual eccentricity. The citizens of the town are embarrassed by them and look upon them as some sort of public disgrace, begrudging them the indispensable cup of chocolate when they call—it's so expensive these days! At least Montenegro has the good grace never to accept. Montenegro falls head over heels for a snobbish girl, a "wind-up doll" who scorns him because of his shabby clothes. Doña Isabel wants to intervene, for poor Montenegro is wasting away with a broken heart. Don Braulio fortuitously receives some money from the estate of a nephew who went to America, which he uses to help the lad.

A prominent citizen of the town gives an elegant party, to which the three friends are invited. Montenegro arrives, elegantly dressed. The girls change their minds about him, but he chides them for their superficiality. He tells a fantastic story about receiving his money from the "Queen of Saxony," who has turned his hair and beard to gold. He has gone completely mad and wanders about tearing the "gold" from his beard. Later he is found dead. Doña Isabel dies, having caught cold in the rain; the cat dies soon after. Don Braulio grieves for his friends and provides for Montenegro's mother. *Ruinas* is a whimsical caricature of types and society, done with gentle humor tinged with pathos. Rosalía's sympathies lie with the humble and sincere, and society is seen as hypocritical and destructive.

C. *"El cadiceño. Descripción de un tipo"*
   ("The Man from Cádiz. Description of a Type")

This brief sketch, first published in *Almanaque de Galicia* in Lugo in 1866, deals with the pernicious social phenomenon of the *cadiceño*, the Galician who goes to southern Spain or to America (through the port of Cádiz) and returns, not much richer than he left, to try to impress the folks back home with his wealth, refinement, and exotic adventures. Two men return to Galicia from Cádiz. They arrive with a great show of baggage and are smoking huge Havana cigars. They flaunt their phony "southern accents" (here Rosalía comically imitates a garbled Andalusian accent) and mock local customs. They generously distribute gifts and souvenirs from their travels—which they bought in local shops. Their trunks are opened before a breathless crowd of family and friends, but they turn out to contain only gaudy souvenirs, secondhand clothes, a real photograph, and other trinkets. Finally, the last trunk, which contains the money, is opened in secret. From a hidden compartment the *cadiceño*, with pathetic bravado, takes out a small bag containing a handful of gold and silver coins. Then the author makes her point, which is a criticism of the foolishness and fakery of those who, having debased themselves for quick profit, take on a veneer of manners representing the worst of the lands they have visited and look down on their own people.

VII *Nonfiction*

A. *"Lieders"* ("Songs") and *"Las literatas"* ("Literary Women")

These two articles, *"Lieders"* (*Album del Miño*, Vigo, 1858), and *"Las literatas"* (*Almanaque de Galicia*, Lugo, 1866), are of interest because of their personal tone and references to the status of women. *"Lieders"* (German for "songs") dates from the same early period as the volume of poetry *La flor* (1857), and contains similar themes. Emotional, rebellious, and resentful, the author defies "the chains of slavery" which are "the patrimony of woman" (1524) and declares herself free and equal. In words strikingly similar to those of the seventeenth-century poet Sor Juana Inés de la Cruz (and perhaps derived from that source), Rosalía reproaches men for causing women to transgress, and then despising them for it. She goes on to speak of remorse and spectral memories which, because of a moment of weakness and fleeting pleasure, follow a woman throughout life.

"Lieders" raises the same intriguing question in the mind of the reader as did the poems of *La flor:* what and whose moment of weakness? Is she sympathizing with women's condition in general, making reference to her mother's misfortune, or alluding to an incident of her own experience? As in the poetry, the anguish and bitterness expressed here are intense and very real.

"Las literatas" ("Literary Women") takes the form of a letter which the author claims to have found and taken the liberty of publishing because the sentiments agree with her own. It dates from the same period as *El caballero de las botas azules* (1867) and expounds similar themes. It is also reminiscent of some of the speeches of Mara in the novel *Flavio* (1861). In the letter a woman called Nicanora addresses a friend, Eduarda, who aspires to be a writer. Her advice is—don't! The writing craze which has seized the country is a plague: "The muses have gone wild. There are more books than the sea has sand, more geniuses than the sky has stars and more critics than there are weeds in the fields." (*"Las musas se han desencadenado. Hay más libros que arenas tiene el mar, más genios que estrellas tiene el cielo y más críticos que hierbas hay en los campos."* 1526).

Futhermore, a woman writer is subject to constant torment.

(Here Rosalía reveals some of her own experiences as a woman writer.) People point at you in the street and gossip about you. If you speak out in a gathering, you are called "*bachillera*" ("know-it-all" or "over-educated"); if you are reserved, they think you are a snob. If you frequent society, you are a show-off; if you don't, you are eccentric. In short, both the women and the men will criticize and shun you (1528–29).

This will ruin your chances for marriage, for men consider a talented woman a calamity. If you are already married, your husband will get the credit—or the blame—for your works. After all, if the work has any merit it must be he who writes it! If he is not an author, pushing you to be famous, but an ordinary man, then the public will think you wear the pants in the family and control him like a puppet. Even though two reasonable people scorn such absurd tales, the reputation of husband and household may suffer. All in all, it doesn't make for a happy life, so think it over, concludes the letter. Feminine awareness, particularly with regard to intellectual and artistic freedom and equality, is a constant theme throughout Rosalía's works. "*Las literatas*" is one of the most direct and vehement expressions of it. In spite of the thin disguise as someone else's letter, the statements give an indication of some of the frustrations she herself had to endure and reveal her sympathy for the position of men who were also victims of narrow minded society.

B. "*Domingo de Ramos*" ("Palm Sunday") and "*Padrón y las inundaciones*" ("Padrón and the Floods") are articles which exemplify Rosalía's lyrical prose style, which combines keen observation and vivid detail with subjective overtones, and her concern for Galician subjects. "*Domingo de Ramos*" ("Palm Sunday") was appended to the novel *El primer loco* (1881). It is not a part of the novel, but relates to it thematically in that it is an example of folk tradition which the author finds beautiful and spiritually meaningful. Lyrically and nostalgically, she describes the festivities and religious observances of Palm Sunday. She remarks on the simple poetry of tradition and faith and contemplates the sadness of life which is occasionally alleviated by collective gaiety. Those like herself, beset by doubt, "inseparable companion of searching spirits tormented by immortal desires . . ." ("*inseparable compañera de los espíritus cavilosos y atormentados por inmortales deseos . . .*" 1498) can derive a measure of peace by joining in the mood of the ceremony.

"*Padrón y las inundaciones*" ("Padrón and the Floods"), published in *La Ilustración Gallega y Asturiana,* Madrid, 1881, was occasioned by destructive floods which at that time threatened Padrón. Rosalía recalls the legend of an ancient city which once sat there, supposedly now at the bottom of a lake. She attributes the flooding of the town to a lack of public works and neglect, and laments that Galicia, so forgotten by the rest of Spain, is neglected as well by its own natives.

VIII *Summation*

Rosalía's prose does not equal her poetry in artistic qualities, yet it is not without its merits and presents some interesting aspects to the modern reader. It offers a wide diversity of styles and subjects and contains an odd mixture of the literary trends of the nineteenth century with large doses of the author herself. It reveals further dimensions of the author which are integral to an understanding of her total literary production. Romanticism is strongly evident, particularly in the early works, which are characterized by exceptional characters, extraordinary events, powerful emotions, dramatic or melancholy depiction of nature, and opulent style. Rosalía frequently mentions her admiration for E. .T. A. Hoffmann, George Sand, Mikhail Lermontov, Lord Byron, and other outstanding Romantic authors, and some of her ideas and techniques could be traced to them. As she and the century advance, traces of Romanticism linger in her subjective approach, rebellious spirit, and pursuit of ideal beauty, but tendencies more in line with Realism can be noted. There is a direct confrontation with contemporary issues and a satirical flaying of social injustices and stupidities.

It is in her prose that Rosalía can be seen to be a woman of her times, an aspect of her identity which alters the usual image of her as the melancholic recluse or dreamer. It is in prose that she enunciates her impatience with the status quo and pleads for change. Her overt statements of protest against attitudes toward women and incisive views on contemporary literature are found in her novels, articles, and prefaces. Although they reflect the age, her prose works cannot be tagged as typical. Rosalía does not fit any mold, and the imprint of her own personality provides a strong unifying element. Certain themes are consistent throughout: fascination with the poetic temperament and the creative process, psychological experience, spiritual versus tangible realities, and search for identity and authenticity. Lyrical qualities prevail; the fiction makes poetic rather than literal sense.

Three of the novels show certain similarities: *La hija del mar* (*Child from the Sea*, 1859); *Flavio* (1861); and *El primer loco* (*The First Madman*, 1881). *La hija del mar* is the most Romantic, which is natural considering its date and the age of the author (twenty-two). The characters are subject to fate (or the author's whims), and the plot is imaginative, complicated, and catastrophic. It most resembles a long poetic narrative or an opera, where credibility does not come into question, but emotional and poetic truths are uppermost. The reader almost expects to hear a musical leit-motif associated with each character. In the character of Teresa, however, can be found a foreshadowing of the tortured souls of the subsequent novels—Flavio, Mara, and Luis.

Flavio and *El primer loco* both shrug at mundane reality as well, but have simpler plots. The focus is on sentimental-psychological drama, with few characters and subdued settings. The characters represent the Romantic temperament, but the author is viewing them from considerable esthetic distance and counterbalances the idealistic and impulsive personalities with forces from the circumstantial and rational world. Mara of *Flavio* and Pedro of *El primer loco* serve this function. They are appreciative and even desirous of flights of fancy, delirium, or insanity, yet nevertheless they retain a firm hold on reality. Mara is the most interesting and best developed character of Rosalía's fiction. Although an idealist and a poet, she is not quite mad, and that is her problem. Whereas the Romantic types are ruled by the heart, subject to the spontaneity of their passions, Mara's mind can never allow her heart to rule absolutely. She is torn between idealism, creativity, and rebelliousness on the one hand and fierce integrity and rational intellect on the other. Her drama is the struggle to reconcile these opposing forces. Idealism and perfect love, incarnated by Flavio, are disappointed. The price of his love is enslavement, annihilation of identity and will, which she cannot accept.

The endings of these three novels are sad, and leave conflicts unresolved. The passive, instinctive characters die, usually after a period of insanity (Esperanza and Luis); a variation is Flavio's "cop-out" of decadence and cynicism. Those that survive and cope (Teresa and Mara) are left bereft and alone. It is up to the reader's imagination to continue their stories. Teresa stands on the shore as her child Esperanza is washed out to sea; Mara, disillusioned with love and dreams, must live on in a stifling world. The solution or consolation of religion is absent.

El caballero de las botas azules (*The Gentleman of the Blue Boots,* 1867) stands apart from the other novels. Notwithstanding its element of fantasy, it is most representative of later-century trends. It departs from the introspective and lyrical and enters a realm of the fancifully grotesque which mocks the shallow and self-complacent values and mannerisms of its time. In the preface *"Un hombre y una musa"* ("A Man and a Muse") Rosalía sets forth an artistic declaration of independence: leave off with the old and trite and get on with the new. The duke in the novel, masculine counterpart of the muse, blasts all the sacred cows of late nineteenth-century Spanish urban society. Passages of *El caballero de las botas azules* can still be read with pleasure, being as fresh and vivid as Dickens, Balzac, Larra, or Galdós. Its spoof of conventions and vanities remains pertinent. In this novel, Rosalía's little-known talent as a humorist is most apparent. The work deserves to be more widely known; there is no other quite like it in Spain's period of Realism.

Even in her earliest, most juvenile efforts, and in a time which preferred hearts and flowers from women writers, Rosalía's prose never falls into the merely pretty nor teaches sugary moralistic lessons. There is an underlying fiber of strength and substance. Her characters, like herself, are nonconformists, rebelling against the so-called morality of appearances and social pressures. Their dramas cannot be contained within proprieties. "Honor" to them is integrity—not "What will the neighbors think?" They are misfits in a society which will not allow natural behavior and realization of self and in which women are left to the mercy of men and a rigid set of rules. She offers no easy solutions, but deals with life in all its contradictions. Selfishness and hypocrisy are her real villains; truth, liberty, and beauty her ideals. Her abhorrence of the hackneyed and false and scorn for middle class values relate her both to Romanticism and Modernism. The lack of the Christian element and search for meaning within the self and the dream relate her more to the later movements and to our own century.

As in the poetry, the underlying theme of Rosalía's prose could well be stated as *dolor*. Love is tragic and impossible, the ideal cannot be realized, the absolute is veiled, consciousness is sickness, the individual is solitary and alienated, and life brings spiritual as well as physical suffering. The element of humor is not dissonant, for humor arises from the perception of the bitter incongruity between the desirable and the actual, the awareness of the tragicomic pathos of humanity. The greatest Spanish tragedies—*El libro de buen amor (The Book of Good Love), La Celestina, Don Quixote*— are also the greatest works of Spanish humor. *Amor con dolor y con humor* (Love with sorrow and humor) might sum up the Spanish outlook on the human dilemma, the fullest expression of the "tragic sense of life."

CHAPTER 9

Conclusion

ROSALÍA de Castro is now regarded as one of the major poets of the nineteenth century in Spain, sharing the distinction with Gustavo Adolfo Bécquer. The importance of their works transcended their own century and has acquired increasing significance in the twentieth. Contemporary critics begin the modern period of Spanish literature with Bécquer and Rosalía, considering them precursors of the Modernists and the Generation of 1898.[1]

Rosalía's early poetic efforts, *La flor* (*The Flower*, 1857) and *A mi madre* (*To My Mother*, 1863), are subjective in content and in style bear strong traces of Romantic models. *Cantares gallegos* (*Galician Songs*, 1863) was her first important book. The poems of *Cantares*, inspired by her love and nostalgia for her homeland, combine the perfectly assimilated Galician tradition with conscious artistry. She recalled popular refrains and elaborated upon them with original variations, keeping faithfully the folk spirit and language. The identity of the poet is subordinate to the collective identity, but her presence is felt in the selection and interpretation of themes and the intensity of emotion. True to Galicia, she is not untrue to herself, for what are to be her constant affinities and preoccupations can be detected behind the mask of the tribal singer.

Cantares was a timely book. It was in line with the Romantic and Realistic interest in the regional and typical, and elicited favorable reactions from established contemporary writers such as Fernán Caballero and Emilia Pardo Bazán. The enthusiasts of Galician cultural and political autonomy of the then very active Galician Restoration movement recognized in Rosalía a talented representative of the region's identity and cultural aspirations. Galicians adored her and claimed her as their own. She became a symbol of their land and heritage and her poems are widely known and loved to this day by Galicians everywhere.

Follas novas (*New Leaves*, 1880) was also written in Galician and retained some traditional themes, but represented a return to subjectivity and a search for personal artistic directions. Guided by the muse of sorrow, the poet entered the labyrinth of her innermost spiritual world, whose contents must be expressed symbolically. The poetic idiom becomes charged with images and the rhythms are vague, suggestive, and complex, fluctuating with mood and theme. *Follas* is the saga of a troubled soul which undertakes the search for psychic wholeness and the meaning of existence.

En las orillas del Sar (*On the Banks of the River Sar*, 1884) is, on one level, a continuation of *Follas*, another stage of the anguished spiritual journey, but marked changes can be noted in the directions of restraint, harmony, and peace. *The Sar*, Rosalía's last work and highest poetic achievement, is in Castilian, addressed to a worldwide public. The basic preoccupations center on the enigma of human existence and destiny, but the tone is less anguished, less desperate. The images and symbols assume more positive values, indicating a progression toward light, hope, and renewal. Stylistic techniques, as well as being adapted to the difference in language, can be seen as a further development of an individualistic poetic medium. As in *New Leaves*, forms obey the impulses of meaning and emotional intensity rather than predetermined molds. *The Sar* represents the apex of Rosalía's poetic and spiritual trajectory. It culminates in a mystical fusion of dream-art-divinity, the jubilant affirmation of all that is creative and transcendent in man.

Follas novas and *En las orillas del Sar* received little attention in Rosalía's time and for many years thereafter. Her reputation as a regionalist and the fame of *Cantares gallegos* overshadowed her more intimate and original works. The later books were considered melancholy and pessimistic and their irregular and intricate rhythms seemed awkward and dissonant. It remained for a later, more rebellious, introspective, and psychologically aware age to penetrate and appreciate the depth and power of Rosalía's best poetry.

As Modernism and the Generation of 1898 emerged at the end of the nineteenth century and beginning of the twentieth, the young poets who were breaking away from Realism and reacting against their immediate predecessors retained their admiration for Bécquer and Rosalía. They held *Cantares gallegos* in high esteem for its interpenetration of author and region, its effortless rendition of traditional poetic forms, and its authentic expression of a facet of the soul of Spain. The solitary and tragic aura which surrounded Rosalía was also compatible with their own temperaments. That part of her work which most nearly resembled their own—*Follas novas* and *En las orillas del Sar*—did not directly influence them in their formative years. For a time the splendor of Rubén Darío and French and other foreign currents dominated the literary scene. When the Modernist tumult had subsided and more interiorized directions became established, the new generation of writers recognized its affinities to Rosalía and she came into her own. Many similarities can be noted in themes, techniques, and imagery between the works of Rosalía and those of Unamuno, Antonio Machado, Azorín, Juan Ramón Jiménez, Valle-Inclán, and Fernando Pessoa, yet these later writers are not her offspring but rather her siblings.

Rosalía's prose has remained obscure and without repercussion among subsequent writers. It reflects the transitional character of her epoch, where prolongations of Romanticism mingle with aspects of Realism. Her prose is difficult to classify, for it is typical of neither movement. The elements absorbed from other authors and from the cultural milieu are uniquely assimilated. Like the poetry, the novels tend to be introverted, preoccupied with the sentimental and psychological experiences of the characters. They project the author's own inner conflicts into fictional personages and symbols. An exception to this generalization is *El caballero de las botas azules (The Gentleman of the Blue Boots),* a fantasy-satire which is extroverted, witty, and topical. Rosalía's prose could offer numerous selected passages of lyrical beauty, dramatic intensity, psychological perspicacity, and delightful humor. For a more complete understanding of her multifaceted and complex literary personality, study of the prose is essential.

The works of Rosalía de Castro contain depths of beauty and meaning which are difficult—or impossible—to exhaust. This brief presentation must close with ellipses. There is always more . . .

Notes and References

Chapter One

1. Henry Levin, *The Gates of Horn. A Study of Five French Realists* (New York, 1966), p. 85.

Chapter Two

1. José Martínez Ruiz [Azorín], *El paisaje español visto por los españoles*, 5th ed. (Madrid, 1959), p. 23.

2. For background information and detailed description of the pilgrimage route and Santiago see James A. Michener, *Iberia. Spanish Travels and Reflections* (New York, 1968), pp. 715–95.

3. For recent accounts of conditions in Galicia, see: Michener; José Yglesias, *The Goodbye Land* (New York, 1967); José María Castroviejo, *Galicia. Guía espiritual de una tierra*, 2nd ed. rev. (Madrid, 1970).

4. Ramón del Valle-Inclán, *Jardín umbrío*, 2nd ed. (Madrid, 1960), p. 65.

5. These collections of medieval poetry were not known in Rosalía's time. Fragmentary editions of the *Cancioneiro da Ajuda* had been published in 1824, 1847, and 1849, but were not widely disseminated and did not influence the poets of the Galician Restoration. The first complete critical editions were: *Cancioneiro da Vaticana*, Ernesto Monaci, ed. (Halle, 1875); *Cancioneiro da Biblioteca Nacional*, Enrico Moltini, ed. (Halle, 1880); *Cancioneiro da Ajuda*, Carolina Michaëlis de Vasconcelos, ed. (Halle, 1904).

6. See the discussion of "Galician-Portuguese Poetry" and "The Great Cancioneiros" in John Esten Keller, *Alfonso X, El Sabio*, (New York, 1967), pp. 96–101.

7. Manuel Murguía, *Galicia* (Barcelona, 1888), p. viii.

8. For bibliography of recent works by noted Galician scholars see Gustavo Fabra Barreiro, *Literatura gallega*, vol. 32 of *Literatura española en imágenes* (Madrid, 1973), p. 64.

Chapter Three

1. The exact wording of Rosalía's birth certificate can be found in Victoriano García Martí, "Rosalía de Castro o el dolor de vivir," which prefaces

his edition of her *Obras completas*, 6th ed. (Madrid, 1966), pp. 15–16, n. 1. The original document is kept in the Hospital Real of Santiago.

2. Some sources maintain that Rosalía was cared for in Ortuño by the servant who acted as her godmother, María Francisca Martínez. See García Martí, p. 16, n. 1; and Benito Varela Jácome, ed., *Rosalía de Castro, Obra poética* (Barcelona, 1972), p. 15. María Francisca was apparently a servant of the Castro family and may also have been a relative of the father's. Marina Mayoral (*La poesía de Rosalía de Castro* [Madrid, 1974]), states that María Francisca Martínez continued in Rosalía's service until after 1859, and that Rosalía was raised by her paternal aunt, Doña Teresa Martínez Viojo (pp. 572–73).

3. Varela Jácome (p. 16) gives the name of this relative as Doña María Josefa García-Lugin.

4. Manuel Murguía, "*La flor*. Poesías de la señorita Rosalía de Castro," *La Iberia* (Madrid), May 12, 1857.

5. Historical and critical works include: *Diccionario de escritores gallegos* (Vigo, 1862); *Historia de Galicia*, 3 vols. (Lugo, 1865; Lugo, 1866; La Coruña, 1888); *Los precursores* (La Coruña, 1886); *Galicia* (Barcelona, 1888). Novels: *Desde el cielo*, 1850, later published with the title *El ángel de la muerte*, 1857; *Oliva*, 1859; *La mujer de fuego*, 1859.

6. S[ylvanus] Griswold Morley, trans., *"Beside the River Sar." Selected Poems from "En las orillas del Sar" by Rosalía de Castro* (Berkeley, 1937). A photograph of the Murguía family in 1884 appears facing page 124.

7. Manuel Murguía, *Los precursores* (La Coruña, 1866; Buenos Aires, 1940), p. 140.

8. Sources do not agree on the birth dates of Rosalía's children except for Alejandra, 1859. Those encountered most frequently are given in the text. A recent and responsible source, Mayoral's *La poesía de Rosalía de Castro*, gives the following birth dates: Aura, 1868; Gala and Ovidio, 1871; Amara, 1873; Adriano Honorato Alejandro, 1875; Valentina, 1877 (p. 580).

9. Three unpublished manuscripts were destroyed at Rosalía's request before her death: *Romana (proverbio)* (*Romana, a Proverb*); "Cuento extraño" ("Strange Tale"); *Historia de mi abuelo* (*Story of My Grandfather*). These works were written before 1862.

10. García Martí, pp. 118–28.

11. Ibid., p. 121.

12. Ibid., p. 123.

13. Rosalía de Castro, *Obras completas*, recopilación y estudio biobibliográfico "Rosalía de Castro o el dolor del vivir" por V. García Martí, 6th ed. (Madrid, 1966), p. 411. All citations of the works of Rosalía are from this edition and will hereafter be indicated by page numbers in the text.

14. Reproductions of photographs and portraits of Rosalía may be found in: *Obras completas*; Morley; Fabra Barreiro; and Augusto Gonzáles Besada, *Rosalía Castro. Notas biográficas* (Madrid, 1916).

15. González Besada, pp. 34–35.

16. Ibid., p. 35.
17. The prevalent use of Rosalía's family name rather than her married name is consistent with Spanish custom. Upon marriage, the woman retains her maiden name and attaches her husband's to it with *de* (of). Among close acquaintances, or if she or her family are well known, she continues to be referred to familiarly by her original name. The married name is affixed in formal or official situations. Rosalía signed her name on her letters and literary compositions as "Rosalía Castro de Murguía."

Chapter Four

1. Quoted by García Martí, p. 68.
2. See note 13 to Chapter 3.

Chapter Five

1. José Luis Varela, *Poesía y restauración cultural de Galicia en el siglo XIX* (Madrid, 1958), p. 20.
2. Rosalía included a glossary of Galician words with *Cantares gallegos* which appears in her *Obras completas*, pp. 382–89. See also Kathleen K. Kulp, *Manner and Mood in Rosalía de Castro: A Study of Themes and Style* (Madrid, 1968), pp. 393–97; X. Luis Franco Grande, *Diccionario galego-castelán y vocabulario castelán–galego* (Vigo, 1968); Leandro Carré Alvarellos, *Diccionario galego-castelán* (La Coruña, 1972); Eladio Rodríguez González, *Diccionario enciclopédico gallego-castellano* (Vigo, 1962).
3. See note 5 to Chapter 2.
4. "Antología del folklore musical de España interpretada por el pueblo español," made by Professor M. García Matos under the auspices of the International Council of Music UNESCO (Madrid: Hispanavox, 1970).
5. For an account of the legend, description of the stones, and photographs of the balanced rock and the chapel of Nuestra Señora de la Barca, see Castroviejo, pp. 551–54.
6. See: Dom Duarte, Infante de Portugal (1391–1438), *Leal conselheiro e livro de ensinança de bem cavalgar tôda sela*, Joseph M. Piel, ed. (Lisbon, 1942); Joaquim Pereira Teixeira de Vasconcelos [Teixeira de Pascoais] (1878–1952), Portuguese poet and creator of an esthetic theory called *saudosismo;* Carolina Michaëlis de Vasconcelos, *A saudade portuguêsa*, 2nd ed. (Pôrto, 1922); and Ramón Piñeiro, "Factores esenciales de la literatura gallega," *Insula* XIV: 152–53 (July-August, 1959), 13.

Chapter Six

1. "Conto gallego" was published by Manuel de Castro y López in *Almanaque Gallego* (Buenos Aires) in 1923. It was later collected by Fermín Bouza Brey in *Cuadernos de Estudios Gallegos* (Santiago de Compostela), II (1946), 279–94. It also appears in Rosalía de Castro, *Contos do pobo* (Vigo, 1970). It is not included in the edition cited of her *Obras completas*.

2. Fernando Pessoa, *Obra poética*, organização, introdução e notas de Maria Aliete Galhoz (Rio de Janeiro, 1965), p. 101.

3. Jolande Jacobi, ed., *The Psychology of C. G. Jung*, foreword by Dr. Jung, 6th ed., new revised (New Haven and London, 1962), p. 59.

4. For traditional or essential meanings of symbols, consult: Juan Eduardo Cirlot, *A Dictionary of Symbols*, translated from the Spanish by Jack Sage, foreword by Herbert Read (New York, 1962); and Carl Gustav Jung, ed., *Man and His Symbols* (Garden City, N.Y., 1964).

5. Blaise Pascal, *Pensées*, texte de l'édition Brunschvicg, introduction et notes par Charles-Marc des Granges (Paris, 1961), Pensée 72, p. 87.

6. Castroviejo gives a description and history of the Torres del Oeste, pp. 132–37, photographs on p. 133 and p. 136.

7. Ramón del Valle-Inclán, *La lámpara maravillosa* (Buenos Aires, 1948), p. 69.

Chapter Seven

1. César Barja, *Libros y autores modernos* (Madrid, 1925), p. 520.

2. Henry Miller, "Un être étoilique," in *A Casebook on Anaïs Nin*, Robert Zaller, ed. (New York, 1974), pp. 7–8. (Italics the author's.)

3. Pessoa, p. 101.

4. Carlos Bousoño, *Teoría de la expresión poética*, 3rd ed. (Madrid, 1962), pp. 128–30.

5. See also the poem "Cenicientas las aguas . . ." ("Ashen are the waters . . ."), *Obras completas*, p. 600.

6. Cirlot, p. 76.

7. See also the poem "Camino blanco, viejo camino, . . ." ("White Road, Old Road, . . ."), *Obras completas*, p. 603.

8. This statue of saint and angel, by José Ferreiro Suárez (1738–1830), has been compared to the St. Teresa of Bernini. See Castroviejo, p. 71.

Chapter Eight

1. José F. Montesinos, *Introducción a una historia de la novela en España en el siglo diecinueve* (Madrid, 1966), p. 35.

2. Ángel del Río, *Historia de la literatura española*, vol. 2 (New York, 1948), p. 89.

3. See note 5 to Chapter 5.

4. Marina Mayoral, "¿Un 'recuerdo encubridor' en Rosalía de Castro?" *Insula* XXIV, nos. 275–76 (October-November, 1969), 1, 12–13.

5. Murguía, *Los precursores*, pp. 148–51.

6. *Los precursores*, p. 150.

7. See note 1 to Chapter 6.

Chapter Nine

1. See Ricardo Gullón, *Direcciones del modernismo* (Madrid, 1963), pp. 7–26.

Selected Bibliography

PRIMARY SOURCES

Primary bibliography is not annotated with evaluations or similar commentary, but an indication of the contents of certain collections and special editions is given because of its usefulness for the reader.

1. Works by Rosalía de Castro in order of publication

La flor. Madrid: M. González, 1857.

"Lieders." *Album del Miño.* Vigo, 1858.

La hija del mar. Vigo: Imprenta de Juan Compañel, 1859; Buenos Aires: Editorial Universal, 1945.

Flavio. Ensayo de novela. Madrid: Imprenta La Crónica de Ambos Mundos, 1861.

Cantares gallegos. Vigo: Imprenta de Juan Compañel, 1863; Nueva edición corregida y aumentada, Leocadio López, ed., Madrid: Imprenta Rivadeneyra, 1872; Madrid: Sucesores de Hernando, 1909; Madrid: Editorial Páez, n.d.; Santiago de Compostela: Librería Gali, n.d.; Buenos Aires: Editorial Tor, 1939; Reedición de la primera edición del año 1863, Santiago de Compostela: Imprenta Librería del Seminario, 1941; Valencia: Tipografía Artística, 1957; Edición del centenario, Fermín Bouza Brey, ed., Vigo: Editorial Galaxia, 1963, 1970; Ricardo Carballero Calero, ed., Salamanca: Anaya, 1963; and Madrid: Ediciones Cátedra, 1974.

A mi madre. Vigo: Imprenta de Juan Compañel, 1863; reproduced in *El Eco de Santiago,* 1926.

"Conto gallego. Os dous amigos e a viuda" (c. 1863). *Almanaque Gallego* (Buenos Aires), 1926, pp. 95–104; and in *Cuadernos de Estudios Gallegos* (Santiago) fascicle 6 (1946), 279–94; included in *Rosalía de Castro: Contos do pobo,* Vigo: Edicións Castrelos, 1970.

Ruinas. Desdichas de tres vidas ejemplares. Vigo: Imprenta de Juan Compañel, 1864; serialized in *El Museo Universal* (Madrid), February, March, April, 1866; Editada con un prefacio por Armando Cotarelo Valador, La Coruña; Imprenta Moret, 1928; Madrid: Imprenta Dédalo, 1943.

137

"El cadiceño. Descripción de un tipo." *Tipos de Galicia* (El Ferrol), 1866; *Almanaque de Galicia* (Lugo), 1866; *El Correo Gallego* (El Ferrol), 1883; *Album de Galicia, El Norte de Galicia* (Lugo), 1916.

"Las literatas." *Almanaque de Galicia* (Lugo), 1866.

El caballero de las botas azules. Lugo: Soto Freire, 1867; Madrid: Sucesores de Hernando, 1911; Barcelona: Editora Juventud, 1931; Buenos Aires: Editorial Emecé, 1942.

Follas novas. Prólogo de Emilio Castelar, Madrid-Habana: Biblioteca de la Propaganda Literaria, 1880; Madrid: Sucesores de Hernando, 1910; Madrid: Editorial Páez, 1933; Buenos Aires: Editorial Emecé, 1943; First edition plus the poem "Un-ha boda na aldea," Vigo: Edicións Castrelos, 1968.

El primer loco. Cuento extraño. Accompanied by the narration "El Domingo de Ramos." Lugo: n.p., 1881; Madrid: Imprenta Moya y Plaza, 1881.

"Padrón y las inundaciones." *La Ilustración Gallega y Asturiana* (Madrid), February 28, March 8, 18, 28, 1881; *Cuadernos de Estudios Gallegos* (Santiago), vol. 2, fascicle 5 (1946), 112–26.

En las orillas del Sar. Madrid: Est. Tipográfico Ricardo Fe, 1884; Prólogo de Manuel Murguía, Epílogo de J. Barcia Caballero y Enrique Díez-Canedo, Madrid: Sucesores de Hernando, 1909; Madrid: Editorial Páez [1925?]; Buenos Aires: Editorial Emecé, 1941; J. Alonso Montero, ed., Salamanca: Anaya, 1964.

2. Lost works

Romana (proverbio); "Cuento extraño"; Historia de mi abuelo.

3. Editions of *Obras completas*

Madrid: Sucesores de Hernando, 6 vols., 1909–1911.

Madrid: Editorial Páez, 1933. Prólogo de Emilio Castelar.

Madrid: Aguilar, 1944, 1947, 1952, 1960, 1966. Prólogo de Victoriano García Martí.

4. Collections

"Beside the River Sar." *Selected Poems from "En las orillas del Sar" by Rosalía de Castro.* Tr. by S[ylvanus] Griswold Morley. Berkeley: University of California Press, 1937.

Cinco poesías de Rosalía de Castro. Publicadas por la Real Academia Española. Madrid: Sucesores de Rivadeneyra, 1900.

Escolma de Poesías de Rosalía de Castro. Selection and preface by Aurelio Ribalta. Barcelona: Editorial Ibérica, 1917.

Las mejores poesías. Prólogo, traducción y selección de Augusto Casas. Barcelona: n.p., 1946.

Obra poética. Estudio y selección por el profesor D. Augusto Cortina. Madrid: Espasa-Calpe, 1946, 1963.

Obra poética. (Bilingüe.) Antología, estudio preliminar, traducción de los poemas gallegos y bibliografía de Don Benito Varela Jácome, Catedrático. Barcelona: Editorial Bruguera, 1972.

Poemas galegos. Antología de poesías de Rosalía recopiladas y prologadas por Eduardo Blanco-Amor. Buenos Aires: Edición Centenario Rosalía. Comisión de Homenaje. Federación de Sociedades Gallegas, 1939.
Poesías: "Cantares gallegos," "Follas novas," "En las orillas del Sar." Vigo: Patronato Rosalía de Castro, 1973.
Rosalía de Castro. Contos do Pobo. Vigo: Edicións Castrelos, 1970.

DICTIONARIES AND GRAMMARS OF GALICIAN

Carballo Calero, Ricardo. *Gramática elemental del gallego común.* Vigo: Editorial Galaxia, 1970.
Carré Alvarellos, Leandro. *Diccionario galego-castelán.* La Coruña: Editorial Moret, 1972.
Franco Grande, X. Luis. *Diccionario galego-castelán y vocabulario castelán-galego.* Vigo: Editorial Galaxia, 1968.
Montero, Xesús Alonso. *O que compre saber da lingua galega.* Buenos Aires: Editorial Alborada, 1969.
Rodríguez Gonzáles, Eladio. *Diccionario enciclopédico gallego-castellano.* 3 vols. Vigo: Editorial Galazia, 1964.

SECONDARY SOURCES

ANDERSON, RUTH MATILDA. *Gallegan Provinces of Spain. Pontevedra and La Coruña.* New York: The Hispanic Society of America, 1939. Detailed descriptions of geography, history, customs, and monuments of Rosalía's region of Galicia. Many illustrations. Notes and bibliography.
BARJA, CÉSAR. *Libros y autores modernos.* Madrid: Sucesores de Rivadeneyra, 1925. A respected authority on Spanish literature. Includes good critical discussion of Rosalía.
CARBALLO CALERO, RICARDO. *Historia da literatura galega contemporánea.* Vigo: Galaxia, 1962. Comprehensive work by a noted Galician scholar. Contains much good information on Rosalía.
———, ed. *Cantares gallegos* by Rosalía de Castro. Salamanca: Anaya, 1963; Madrid: Ediciones Cátedra, 1974. Informative introduction and notes.
CASTELAR, EMILIO. "Prólogo," a *Follas novas* de Rosalía de Castro. Madrid: Biblioteca de la Propaganda Literaria, 1880; Madrid: Imprenta de Sucesores de Hernando, 1909. Included in *Obras completas de Rosalía de Castro,* V[ictoriano] García Martí, ed. Madrid: Aguilar, 1944, 1947, 1952, 1960, 1966. Interesting prologue to the first edition of *Follas novas* by a noted nineteenth-century critic and historian.
CASTROVIEJO, JOSÉ MARÍA. *Galicia. Guía espiritual de una tierra.* 2nd ed. rev. Madrid: Espasa-Calpe, 1970. Description, history, impressions of Galicia by a Galician author. Profusely illustrated. Excellent for information on Galicia and background and ambience of Rosalía's works.

CIRLOT, JUAN EDUARDO. *A Dictionary of Symbols*. Tr. by Jack Sage. Foreword by Herbert Read. New York: Philosophical Library, 1962. Comprehensive and scholarly reference work on symbols and their meanings by a noted Spanish art critic and historian.

COUCEIRO FREIJOMIL, ANTONIO. *Diccionario bio-bibliográfico de escritores gallegos*. Santiago de Compostela: Ed. Bibliófilos Gallegos, 1961. Concise sketches of Galician writers.

Cuadernos de Estudios Gallegos. Santiago de Compostela. Journal devoted to Galician studies. Contains many articles on Rosalía and her works by scholars such as Fermín Bouza Brey, Ricardo Carballo Calero, Lázaro Montero, José Luis Varela, and many others.

DA CAL, ERNESTO GUERRA. "Galician literature." In *Encyclopedia of Literature*. New York: Philosophical Library, 1946. Summmary of Galician literature including remarks on Rosalía.

————. "O renascimento galego contemporâneo." *Luso-Brazilian Review* (Madison, Wisconsin) 1, no. 1 (June, 1964), 5–18. Discusses essential qualities of Galician literature and their expression in contemporary writers.

DEL RÍO, ÁNGEL. *Historia de la literatura española*. Vol. 1: *Desde los orígenes hasta 1700;* Vol. 2: *Desde 1700 hasta nuestros días*. New York: Holt, Rinehart and Winston, 1948; New York: Henry Holt and Co., 1960. Sound and readable history of Spanish literature. Vol. 2 gives excellent survey of nineteenth-century literature and includes an appendix on Galician literature.

DÍAZ-PLAJA, GUILLERMO, ed. *Historia general de las literaturas hispánicas*. 5 vols. Barcelona: Editorial Barna, 1957–58. A compilation of authoritative studies. See: Jorge Campos, "El romanticismo," vol. 4, pt. 2; José María de Cossío, "La poesía en la época del naturalismo," vol. 5, pp. 28–31; José Filgueira Valverde, "Lírica medieval gallega y portuguesa," vol. 1, pp. 545–643; Vicente Risco, "La poesía gallega," vol. 4, pt. 2; José Luis Varela, "La prosa en Galicia en el siglo XIX," vol. 4, pt. 2.

FABRA BARREIRO, GUSTAVO. *Literatura gallega*. Vol. 32 of *Literatura española en imágenes*. 32 vols. Madrid: Editorial La Muralla, 1973. Summary of Galician literature with sixty slides including a portrait of Rosalía and a view of her house, "La Matanza." Bibliography.

GARCÍA MARTÍ, V[ICTORIANO]. "Rosalía de Castro o el dolor de vivir." Prologue to *Obras completas de Rosalía de Castro*. 6th ed. Madrid: Aguilar, 1966. Basic source for background, biographical data, and critical appreciation of Rosalía.

GONZÁLEZ BESADA, AUGUSTO. *Rosalía Castro. Notas biográficas*. Madrid: Biblioteca Hispania, 1916. Early biographical study. Contains reproductions of rare portraits.

GULLÓN, RICARDO. *Direcciones del modernismo*. Madrid: Editorial Gredos, 1963. In-depth study of the phenomenon of Modernism and its major figures in which Bécquer and Rosalía are regarded as true forerunners of the movement.

Insula (Madrid) XIV, nos. 152–153 (July-August, 1959). Special issue on Galician literature.

JACOBI, JOLANDE, ed. *The Psychology of C. G. Jung.* Foreword by Dr. Jung. 6th ed. rev. New Haven and London: Yale University Press, a Yale Paperbound, 1962. Lucid condensation of Jungian psychological theories which are helpful in interpreting Rosalía's works.

JUNG, CARL GUSTAV, ed. *Man and his Symbols.* Garden City, New York: Doubleday and Co., 1964. Collection of essays edited by the great psychologist and authority on symbols. Profusely illustrated.

KELLER, JOHN ESTEN. *Alfonso X, El Sabio.* New York: Twayne Publishers, Inc., 1967. Contains excellent information on medieval Galician-Portuguese poetry, pp. 70–73; 96–110.

KULP, KATHLEEN K. *Manner and Mood in Rosalía de Castro: A Study of Themes and Style.* Madrid: Ediciones José Porrua Turanzas, 1968. Comprehensive study of thematic continuity and development and stylistic devices of Rosalía's poetry. Extensive bibliography.

LAPESA, RAFAEL. "Bécquer, Rosalía y Machado." *Insula* IX, nos. 100–101 (1954), 6. Comparative study of three major Spanish poets.

LÁZARO, ÁNGEL. *Rosalía de Castro. Un autor en un libro.* Madrid: Compañía Bibliográfico Española, 1966. General overview of life and works. Chronology and bibliography.

LEVIN, HENRY. *The Gates of Horn. A Study of Five French Realists.* New York: Oxford University Press, 1966. Perceptive study of Realism seen through the works of Stendhal, Balzac, Flaubert, Zola, and Proust. Gives valuable insights into nineteenth-century French prose which can be applied to Spanish literature as well.

MARTÍN, ELVIRA. *Tres mujeres gallegas del siglo XIX. Rosalía de Castro, Concepción Arenal, Emilia Pardo Bazán.* Barcelona: Editorial Aedos, 1962. Presentation of Rosalía along with two other prominent Galician women writers, her contemporaries.

MARTÍNEZ RUIZ, JOSÉ [AZORÍN]. "Rosalía de Castro." In *Clásicos y modernos.* Vol. 2 of *Obras completas de Azorín.* Edited by Ángel Cruz Rueda, pp. 770–75. Madrid: Aguilar, 1959. Essay by a member of the Generation of 1898, one of the first to appreciate Rosalía's significance in modern poetry.

———. *El paisaje español visto por los españoles.* 5th ed. Madrid: Espasa-Calpe, 1959. See Chapter 2, "Galicia," pp. 23–35.

MAYORAL, MARINA. *La poesía de Rosalía de Castro.* Prólogo de Rafael Lapesa. Madrid: Gredos, 1974. Recent and comprehensive study of Rosalía's major themes and stylistic techniques. Extensive bibliography.

————. "¿Un 'recuerdo encubridor' en Rosalía de Castro?" *Insula* XXIV, nos. 275–276 (October–November, 1969), 1, 12–13. Discusses possible allusions to the preoccupation with illegitimacy and absence of father in certain of Rosalía's early poems.

MICHENER, JAMES A. *Iberia. Spanish Travels and Reflections*. 3rd printing. New York: Random House, 1968. Vivid and informative travel account. Of particular interest is Chapter 13, "Santiago de Compostela," pp. 715–95.

MONTERO, J. ALONSO, ed. *En las orillas del Sar* by Rosalía de Castro. Salamanca: Ediciones Anaya, 1964. Informative prologue, notes, chronology, and bibliography.

MONTESINOS, JOSÉ F. *Introducción a una historia de la novela en España en el siglo diecinueve*. Madrid: Castalia, 1966. Survey of the development, influences, and principal tendencies of the Spanish nineteenth-century novel.

MORLEY, S[YLVANUS] GRISWOLD, trans. *"Beside the River Sar." Selected poems from "En las orillas del Sar" by Rosalía de Castro*. Berkeley: University of California Press, 1937. Useful preface and informative notes. Contains reproductions of rare portraits of Rosalía and her family.

MURGUÍA, MANUEL. *Galicia*. Barcelona: Establecimiento Tipográfico-Editorial de Daniel Cortezo y Compañía, 1888. Major historical work by the "patriarch" of the Galician Restoration, Rosalía's husband.

————. "*La flor*. Poesías de la señorita Rosalía de Castro," *La Iberia* (Madrid), May 12, 1857. Review of Rosalía's first book.

————. *Los precursores*. La Coruña: Latorre y Martínez, 1886; Buenos Aires: Emecé, 1940. A collection of critical essays including "Rosalía Castro," pp. 129–151.

————. "Prólogo" to *En las orillas del Sar* by Rosalía de Castro. Madrid: Sucesores de Hernando, 1909. Included in *Obras completas de Rosalia de Castrol*, V. García Martí, ed., pp. 555–67. 6th ed. Madrid: Aguilar, 1966. Critical and personal observations concerning Rosalía.

NOGALES DE MUÑIZ, MARÍA ANTONIA. *Irradiación de Rosalía de Castro. Palabra viva, tradicional y precursora*. Barcelona: Talleres Gráficos Ángel Estrada, 1966. Study of Rosalía's themes, influences, and connection with later poets. Extensive bibliography.

PATTISON, WALTER THOMAS. *Emilia Pardo Bazán*. New York: Twayne Publishers, Inc., 1971. Concise study of an outstanding Galician writer, Rosalía's contemporary. Good observations on Galicia.

PIÑEIRO, RAMÓN. "Factores esenciales de la literatura gallega." *Insula* XIV, nos. 152–153 (July–August, 1959), 13. Discusses basic qualities of Galician literature, including *saudade* and humor.

POULLAIN, CLAUDE HENRI. *Rosalía Castro de Murguía y su obra literaria*. Comprehensive study with good treatment of chronology, themes and metrics of Rosalía's works. Examines similarities with other writers and possible influences. Extensive bibliography.

PRADO COELHO, JACINTO DO. *Dicionário da literatura portuguêsa, brasileira, galega e estilística literária.* 2 vols. Pôrto: Livraria Figuerinhas, 1956–60; 2nd ed., 1969. An excellent reference work on the Lusitanian literatures. Contains an informative entry on Rosalía.

7 [*Siete*] *ensayos sôbre Rosalía.* Vigo: Galaxia, 1952. A collection of critical essays by noted literary figures.

SUÁREZ RIVERO, ELIANA. "Machado y Rosalía: dos almas gemelas." *Hispania* XLIV, no. 4 (December, 1966), 748–51. Comparison of Rosalía and Antonio Machado, prominent poet of the Generation of 1898.

TIRELL, SISTER MARY PIERRE. *La mística de la saudade. Estudio de la poesía de Rosalía de Castro.* Madrid: Ediciones Jura, 1951. Discusses Rosalía's life, influences, and themes. Particularly useful for study of metric forms.

UNAMUNO, MIGUEL DE. *Del sentimiento trágico de la vida.* 5th ed. Buenos Aires-México: Espasa-Calpe Argentina, S. A., 1942. Philosophical study by a famous member of the Generation of 1898 which discusses "the tragic sense of life." Unamuno's thoughts on man and his destiny bear a striking resemblance to Rosalía's.

VALLE-INCLÁN, RAMÓN DEL. *Jardín umbrío.* 2nd ed. Madrid: Espasa-Calpe, 1960. Collection of short stories by a famous Galician writer, member of the Generation of 1898. Set in Galicia, the stories give insights into the legendary and mysterious aspects of Galician culture.

———. *La lámpara maravillosa. (Ejercicios espirituales).* Buenos Aires-México: Espasa-Calpe, S. A., 1948. Reflections on esthetics and philosophy which show many parallels with Rosalía's themes.

VARELA, JOSÉ LUIS. *Poesía y restauración cultural de Galicia en el siglo XIX.* Madrid: Editorial Gredos, 1958. Thorough study of Galician cultural and political activities in the nineteenth century. Extensive notes. Chapter on "Rosalía y la saudade," pp. 145–211.

VARELA JÁCOME, BENITO. "Estudio preliminar" to *Rosalía de Castro, obra poética.* Barcelona: Editorial Bruguera, 1972. Informative introduction. Translation to Spanish of Galician poems. Bibliography.

———. *Historia de la literatura gallega.* Santiago de Compostela: Editorial Porto, 1951.

YGLESIAS, JOSÉ. *The Goodbye Land.* New York: Pantheon Books, 1967. Interesting account by an American writer of Galician descent who visits Spain in search of information on his family. Sensitive impressions of land, people, and life in Galicia.

Index

(The works of Rosalía de Castro are listed under her name)

144